ELEMENTS
OF LIVING™

HARDSCAPING

HIGH STYLE, LOW MAINTENANCE OUTDOOR SPACES

Haig Seferian, ASLA, with Claire Whitcomb

McGraw Hill Professional

The McGraw·Hill Companies

Cataloging-in-Publication Data is on file with the Library of Congress

1 2 3 4 5 6 7 8 9 0 PUR/PUR 0 9 8 7 6 5 4 3 2 1

ISBN 0-07-142249-8.

The sponsoring editor for this book was Cary Sullivan and the production supervisor was Pamela Pelton.

Printed in China by Print Vision.

McGraw-Hill books are available at special quantity discounts to use as premiums and sales promotions,
or for use in corporate training programs. For more information, please write to the Director of Special
Sales, McGraw-Hill, 2 Penn Plaza, New York, NY 10121-2298. Or contact your local bookstore.

The book is printed on acid-free stock.

ELEMENTS
OF LIVING™

Packaged by Elements Media
Creative Director: Chris Kincade
Art Direction/Graphic Design: Boomerang Studio
Editorial Assistant: Gayle Brosnan

Elements of Living is a trademark of Elements Media, LLC.

Elements Media, LLC
16 West 19th Street, Tenth Floor
New York, NY 10011

DEDICATION

For my wife, Marina, and children, Matthew and Zoie, who offer me the greatest joy in life everyday. And to my parents, Boghos and Armenouhi, for encouraging me with my creative path in life.

— Haig

ACKNOWLEDGEMENTS

First and foremost, I would like to thank all of the industry experts, designers, architects, contractors and artisans for sharing their time, knowledge and projects with us. This book would not have been possible without Tony DiGiovanni of Landscape Ontario and the landscape industry that I am so proud and honored to be a part of. Of course, I am equally indebted to Cary Sullivan at McGraw-Hill and Chris Kincade of Elements Media for giving me the opportunity to be a member of the team. My co-author, Claire, also deserves a special mention here because she made my years of knowledge and experience come alive on the page. I'd also like to thank my ever-understanding business partner Norm Sinclair, who picked up the slack at the office to allow me time to prepare this book; David Foster, for his tireless efforts in locating the images for this book; Amanda Enwright of AJE Productions, who gave me the opportunity to host HGTV's *Garden Architecture;* Nazeli and John Claussen for their continued support; William (Bill) DeLuca, my business mentor and good friend; and my good friend and colleague John Bridges. And gardeners worldwide who inspire and allow me to creatively design and bring to fruition their own personal gardens. And finally, much love and thanks to my wife for her patience, help and understanding with this grand endeavor.

TABLE OF CONTENTS

If you follow the proper processes from beginning to end, a landscape
can conjure memories of great vacation spots.

INTRODUCTION

Growing up in an apartment complex in the small city of Hamilton, Ontario, the only exterior spaces immediately available to me were the surrounding parking lot and sidewalks—my first hardscapes. *Outside* was something simply to be passed through, and I envied my friends who lived

in nearby family homes, with their own porches and yards. They experienced the outdoors very differently. To me, it seemed almost like magic to be outside without ever leaving home. I always thought, What a wonderful connection with the world this must be, and I suppose this is where my love of exterior spaces originated.

Since starting my own landscape design business, I've found that seeing these outdoor spaces develop often feels like the same sort of magic to my clients. Hardscaping—the patios, pergolas, walkways, driveways, pools, ponds and other landscaping elements built with hard materials—has a lot to do with that. For many of us, the word "landscaping" conjures up images of lush lawns, garden beds bursting with color and trees in full leaf. In fact, if you're new to landscape design, it may not even occur to you that there's more to it than your lawn, garden beds and trees. Hardscaping is quite often the centerpiece of an outdoor space, and if done well, it sets the stage for the magic to occur. Still, many of us view it as strictly utilitarian.

Just how important is your hardscape? We've all seen pretty garden plots sitting like outposts on an expanse of lawn, with no way to get there and no particular reason—unless you're the gardener—to go. What a difference a simple gravel path would make. That's hardscaping. It guides us through our outdoor spaces and, when designed properly, endures for a lifetime. You can

always rip out a yellow rose bush, but it's difficult to resituate a flight of stairs cut into a rocky slope.

So why do so many of us settle for less than optimal hardscaping solutions? We'll spend days contentedly manicuring our garden, yet often treat the more functional components of our landscapes as an afterthought. In my experience, this is because most of us sim-

Small corners of the garden are perfect for water features or sculptures. Remember that every square foot of your landscape should hold meaning for you and also work in relation to your home.

ply don't understand the wealth of possibilities available.

In *Hardscaping*, I've tried to put together both a simple getting-started process to help you understand all of the opportunities your landscape holds and a clear framework for turning it into a series of truly high style, low maintenance spaces. Because that's what hardscaping is all about. It doesn't need pruning, it doesn't require watering and when your "softscape"—flowers, trees and other vegetation—isn't in full bloom, it's what keeps your yard a useful and pleasant place to be.

For both do-it-yourselfers and those working closely with a landscape architect or designer, *Hardscaping* is an illustrated look at the concepts, techniques and materials you'll want to consider as you re-imagine your landscape. The first chapter, *Designing Outdoor Spaces*, offers a simple framework for under-

Here, natural stone slab steps provide a great blend of high style and low maintenance. Selection of the proper materials for your outdoor spaces should cater to both needs.

Retaining walls are a great blend of form and function. They can create terraces or planting beds out of sloped land and also add texture to the overall look and feel of the surroundings.

The right professionals can help you transform your outdoor space. Here are the three basic types you'll likely encounter:

Landscape architect: A formally trained professional qualified to plan landscapes and public areas of all types, including public, commercial, industrial and residential properties. In most areas, the use of the title is restricted by law to licensed individuals.

Landscape designer: A person with a strong background in horticulture, landscape design, landscape construction and graphics who provides designs for single-family residential landscapes. Not a licensed title, although formal education in the subject area is highly desirable. The same services may be offered by persons operating under other non-licensed titles, e.g., garden designer.

Landscape contractor: A firm or individual licensed to enter into a contract with the client for the installation of new landscapes. Most areas regulate the landscape trade through a licensing procedure.

Courtesy of *The Landscape Design Series Video Teaching Guide.*

standing the design process, while subsequent chapters look at specific elements in your landscape, including outdoor rooms, enclosures, access ways, water features and outdoor decorating. Throughout, a variety of sidebars and design tips have been included to address specific issues you'll encounter. Finally, you'll also find a number of *Materials Quick Tours* that give basic overviews of the materials commonly used in the landscape.

Because installation and maintenance issues for specific parts of your landscape could fill their own books, I've addressed them only when they affect the design process. If these are concerns, you should make sure to speak with appropriate professionals—or, if you're both the designer *and* contractor, consult specific "how-to" books or local building codes on such issues as building gazebos and pool houses.

Think of *Hardscaping* as the first step in building a landscape that caters to your needs, inspires the neighborhood and continues to thrill you, night or day, winter or summer. It should, I hope, help you create your own outdoor magic.

Above: Landscapes set the mood of the home and give a sense of the personality of the homeowners. Stately, surprising and simple are a few tones that you can set through good design.

Opposite: When planning your outdoor spaces, make sure that they reflect the architecture of your home. A country estate should look like a country estate from all angles on the property.

Creating a secret garden is one approach to outdoor design. Interested in what lies beyond, visitors will be drawn through the gate. A soft transition, with overgrown plant material, makes this entrance an informal one.

Waterfalls are best placed on natural grade drops. With proper planting techniques and stone sections, a waterfall can look like a natural feature of the landscape.

A good garden design has elements of mystery and intrigue. Here, the garden is partially revealed in order to draw one further down the path.

CHAPTER 1

DESIGNING OUTDOOR SPACES

People often think design begins with a focus on beauty and style, though nothing could be further from the truth. A designer creates great living spaces outdoors just as he or she does indoors: with a fully developed plan that takes into account the functions and limitations of the space.

Turning your design concepts into successful outdoor living spaces begins with making basic decisions about what activities will take place in each space, who will use them and how the spaces will accommodate the various functions. Even if you're just building a walkway from your driveway to the front door, you should think about whether it needs to accommodate strollers or wheelchairs. More elaborate projects, like a terrace, naturally require more thought: Where do you want to take your morning coffee? How do you want to orient sitting areas with the sun? Will you entertain often? If so, do you tend to plan on dinner parties for six or cocktail parties for thirty?

Asking the right questions is often the most critical part of the design process, and in this chapter, I've outlined a basic method to help you begin that process. If you adhere to the process, plan properly and consult experts as you need them, the result will be a design that meets and most likely exceeds your expectations. You'll also find yourself better equipped to personalize your space, create inspired site-specific details and stylishly integrate outdoor areas with the house, both the interior and exterior.

WHAT'S GOOD ABOUT GOOD DESIGN

Before embarking on your project, set your expectations. Your project shouldn't be about generating any design, but about generating good design. Enduring design. Design that will repay your investment in landscaping. Design that makes people comfortable and at ease. Even though it seems impossible for two people to agree on what is beautiful, there are some formal ways to measure whether your design will meet those criteria.

The elements, principles and form composition concepts described below combine to generate good design.

A single garden space can easily be divided into garden rooms. Walls, ceilings and floors of varying materials create great gateways and transitions.

The elements describe the physical qualities of the design, such as form, color, shape and texture; the principles describe how the elements should be ordered, such as balance, contrast, movement and repetition; and the form composition is the shape the space takes (curved, angular or modular). Understanding these fundamentals will give you a basis for evaluating design and help you identify and articulate aspects of a design that you do and don't like. The more closely your design conforms to these fundamentals, the richer it will be.

Elements & Principles

Mary Palmer Dargan, professor of landscape architecture at Clemson University and a principal of the Atlanta-based firm Dargan Landscape Architects, offers the following descriptions of the elements and principles:

The key to success in garden design is in arranging the property according to the basic tools of visual art. Utilize the four art elements (line, color, form and texture) and the principles of design (focalization, axial geometry, proportion, scale, repetition and rhythm), and you will coax out the very best design for your garden.

Line, color, form and texture are the backbone ingredients in any designer's bag of tricks.

1. **Line** is directional. The "s" curve, or Hogarth's line of beauty, is an element that draws the eye into a picture and adds mystery, such as when you can't quite see around a curve of shrubs, or when winding lines animate the ground plane. A straight line is the quickest way between two points, but it can also be boring.

2. **Color** is emotional. Hot colors, such as red or yellow, bring activity to the foreground. Cool colors like pink, purple or blue cause images to recede. Monochromatic color schemes, such as using bluestone, gray stucco walls and furniture painted a gray-green, tend to make a small space seem larger.

3. **Form** leaves a lasting impression of a shape. Conical evergreens are inspirational and lift your eyes to the heavens, which is why they are often planted in cemeteries. Clipped hedges or topiaries have clearly defined shapes. Less clear but subtler are the undulating forms of flowing contours that offer "soft" bumps throughout a landscape, as opposed to harder geometries.

4. **Texture** leads the eye from voids to solids, all the while making the place lively. Objects in the foreground will look closer if they are coarsely textured. In a tiny courtyard, a maidenhair fern used as

edging will convey a sense of space due to its dainty, finely textured fronds. A diversity of textures (fine, medium, coarse) when mixed together in masses will enliven a space due to the plant texture and the size of space between each. It leads the eye. Likewise, bricks as a border to a gravel walk seem to dominate the finely textured gravel due to their coarse, or large, size.

The following design principles are more subjective and employ the art elements to do their business:

1. **Repetition** is easily recognized by the use of repeated shapes in a rhythm. Bumps of boxwoods spring to mind or street trees lined up along an allée. Walkways are often lined with boxwood or floral edgings that repeat the line of the walk.

2. **Rhythm** involves the spaces and density of the repeated objects and works with repetition as a design principle. The same plant material, such as mounding Japanese maple, can repeat a shape but be scattered throughout the garden in a rhythm.

3-4. **Axial geometry** and **focalization** often go hand in hand due to the dance the line, an art element, imposes. A focal point is a terminal item at the end of a walk, an allee of trees or an arbor, and it draws your view along a centerline.

5-6. **Proportion** and **scale** are design principles best acknowledged by "I know it when I see it." That said, it is important to test all heights of columns, statues, fountain features and the like by placing a simple "mock-up" in the location, standing back and deciding if it fits. Another method is to draw an elevation of the item in its future environment. A scaled drawing is far more cost-effective than a hastily constructed and awkward arbor.

After learning the potentials of the site, a designer can apply these design tools to create a masterpiece. Each garden is as individual as a fingerprint and has its own genetic code. By using the art elements and design principles, a designer can create a living work of art.

From top to bottom: (1) These square flagstones repeat the rhythm of the front walk. (2) The curved bed lines draw the viewer through the garden. The line is a path of action, a powerful tool in a designer's arsenal. (3) Form and shape are essential elements in creating a good design.

Angular compositions are a great choice if your home or yard has angular structures such as a bumped-out breakfast room or a gazebo. These types of structures look best when surrounded by similarly shaped plantings and paths. Another good reason to use angular composition is that it creates the illusion of spaciousness and is often the best solution in long, narrow lots or postage-stamp urban gardens.

Form Composition

Form composition, the shape the space takes, falls into four general categories:

Modular Composition: If everything in your proposed landscape—all of your planting beds, lawns, patio spaces, pools, etc.—has 90-degree corners (i.e., squares and rectangles), then your design is perfectly modular and will work well.

Curvilinear Composition: If everything is curved and nothing has sharp angles, your design is perfectly curvilinear and will work well.

Angular Composition: The 45-degree angle is by far the most common angle used in residential design. If the shapes in your landscape are defined by 45-degree angles, the design is perfectly angular and will work well.

Hybrid Composition: This style of design utilizes two of the three forms of composition listed above. For example, a curved patio set against an angular house.

Here's one of the only rules I'm going to lay down in this book: If your design conforms to one of the first three categories of form composition, it is good design. In other words, it violates no design principles. The same is true if your design combines any two of the first three categories. Combine all three, however, and you've dissolved composition into a free-for-all. Such designs are rarely visually coherent or pleasant.

Above: Curvilinear planting beds are by far the most common form of composition in landscape design. **Opposite:** In this modular design, the water features and associated walls follow all the same rules of form composition. The angular roof is the only accent not designed with right angles.

TYPES OF GARDEN ROOMS

Transforming the yard into a series of "garden rooms" can produce some of the most inviting spaces in which to live and play, so it's important to understand what sort of style and functions are right for you. Here are three simple ways to think about your outdoor living spaces:

A formal garden room: This is a setting in which many aspects of a traditional room are reproduced. Plantings, pergolas or other landscaping materials can be used to define the area and provide an appropriate level of privacy, while pavers can serve as flooring that further distinguishes the space. Accessories and furnishings are then added to enhance the room's functionality, contributing to a distinct, formal space within natural environs. The hallmarks of a formal space are symmetry and a preponderance of straight lines and right angles in its shapes.

A semi-formal garden room: This type of design

Top: The detailing of the pergola and latticework overhead not only provide subtle streams of filtered light but also enclose this formal garden space. **Bottom:** Even as this semi-formal garden room flows easily into the adjoining lawn, the flooring and stone fencing create a sense of enclosure.

carves out a garden room more by suggestion than by enclosure. It may be delineated by partial enclosures, such as planters or half pergolas, that are used to distinguish between two distinct spaces without creating real "walls." This space may not have all the elements of an interior, but it is clearly recognizable as a separate area with its own uses. Curvature and flow characterize the semi-formal room. Although it may be perfectly symmetrical, with bordered flowerbeds, crisply laid walkways, and poured concrete pools, the absence of sharp angles makes it feel more relaxed than its formal counterpart. Perhaps the most familiar example of semi-formal design is the Japanese garden that, despite its rigorous use of exact design modules, always feels natural and serene.

One or two key design elements, such as flooring and furniture, may be all that is needed to demarcate the space.

A natural garden room: This is an outdoor space that integrates with its surroundings rather than seeking to replace them. Where nature has created a sheltered place or sweeping expanse that induces people to stop, sit and reflect, a room of sorts already exists. Adding a human dimension, such as benches or pavers, is all that is required in this type of setting. The use of indigenous materials is vital in order to maintain the aesthetics established by the environment. Each season is a different experience to the occupant of a natural retreat, but the elements of this type of garden should appeal to your sense of smell, touch and sound year-round.

In this natural garden room, decking and outdoor furniture have been added to a secluded waterfront spot to establish an unobtrusive human dimension.

1. What sort of activities will take place in the planned space, and how will those activities affect the design?
2. Who will use the space, and how do these individuals impact the project's needs? Will there be children playing tag, gourmets grilling, guests gathered with wineglasses under the stars?
3. How will sun cycles impact the site and orientation issues? Is there a particularly good corner of the yard to catch the morning sun or an area to watch the sunset in the evening?
4. Which views should be played up, and which should be played down?
5. Are there street noises that should be masked either by walls or the sound of water?
6. Do you need to protect against wind, salt air breezes or rain?
7. How will the project integrate with the house and with the surroundings?
8. How will the changing seasons impact your site and your project?
9. Where are the best places to build, and what are the advantages or disadvantages of each?
10. In what ways are neighboring sites used (by foot or by vehicle), and how will those usage patterns affect your site and project?

NINE STEPS OF PLANNING A LANDSCAPE

Now that you have an idea of what sort of garden experience you'd like to create, you're ready to begin thinking about the design. While the following nine steps do represent a step-by-step process, design is organic, and you'll likely want to incorporate some of the later steps early in the process. For example, you may make easy maintenance (step nine) part of your wish list (step one). So, as you put together your design with your landscape architect, designer or contractors, make sure to come back to these nine steps regularly, and always look ahead to the next steps.

One. Pre-Design & Wish List

Before beginning a design, you need a basic understanding of what you're looking for. Outdoor spaces, even more so than indoor ones, are successful to the degree that they create a sense of place—a tall order sometimes, as open air spaces are, by definition, barely contained. Therefore, two-dimensional diagrams are even less effective than house blueprints at conveying what it would feel like to be in that outdoor place. Thus, you need to become adept at visualizing your design each step of the way.

Photographs of the site help to some extent: Pin them up on a wall to help you focus on certain areas and discover details that you wouldn't normally see standing alongside the property and viewing it as a whole. It's also a good idea to flip through magazines looking for landscape ideas and to get used to viewing spaces from a variety of angles. Consider the view from your front door, your living room window or even the kitchen sink. Think how you see your landscape now and how you could enhance your viewing pleasure with an improved design. If you haven't already done so, go out and experience a variety of garden rooms. Walk into, around and through them, making note of what you like and what you hope to avoid. And be practical: If you find that you love the look of a lot of plants and flowers, ask yourself if you also love getting down on your knees in the garden bed.

Lifestyle is also a critical component of design. The "Lifestyle Questionnaire" (see sidebar) is a good place to begin: It will give you an idea of how your personal preferences can and should impact the design. You should consider how you plan to use the space, and be precise. Do you plan to create a place for reading in a hammock? For taking an outdoor shower? Will you use the space for sitting with a cup of coffee in the morning? If you're building a walkway, will it need to accommodate wheelchairs or strollers? Asking yourself personal questions about your lifestyle will help you assess both your needs and your budget priorities.

A quick word on budgets: This is something clients are often reluctant to discuss, both because they don't have much sense of what things cost and because they want to continue dreaming of fountains and arbors as long as possible. However, if you can come up with a ballpark figure, you will be better able to help set priorities and seek out both a cost-effective and premium solution for almost everything you want to do.

Done well, this critical and highly creative phase of planning will yield fresh ideas and a set of realistic expectations. The next step is setting all your inspirations, ideas and wishes down on paper. Since these are only loosely based on the capabilities of your outdoor space, this is your wish list. Simply sit down and write out a list of things you'd like your new project to provide. (See page 30 for a sample wish list.)

Two. Inventory

Once you have an idea of what you hope to accomplish, you're ready to tackle the actual design. This step involves documenting what you have to work with. A designer will measure the site and record all existing features, which he or she will later use to prepare what is aptly called a base plan that is drawn to scale on a grid. All future design phases will then be drawn on tracing paper that gets layered atop the base plan to reveal potential conflicts and obstacles. For that reason, the base plan should display every element of the existing landscape, including sheds, pavement or pools, even if they're going to be removed. The base plan document will have directional orientation so you'll know how the sun revolves around the property and where sun and shade areas are located. This means that your inventory must include all of these issues. To see what a good base plan and inventory should look like, go to the case study on page 30.

If you're working with a designer, make sure to show them vistas that only appear in certain seasons, and point out trouble spots, such as areas that may turn swampy in a heavy rain or where street noise is too loud at certain times of day. You also may want to find the survey or deed for the property to aid in the base plan development. If you're doing the project on your own and developing your own base plan (see the "DIY Base Plans" sidebar), you'll need to make note of these issues. In this step, it's also important to collect as much information as possible about problems that could be created by sur-

rounding sites. Don't think purely in terms of privacy issues or views you'd like to shield, but look at usage patterns as well: Where does most of the nearby foot traffic take place? Vehicular traffic? In what other ways are the surrounding sites used that may impact your own?

If drafting even a rudimentary base plan seems too large a task, your inventory can be a simple survey of your property. Kira Gould offers some basic questions you should answer as you do your inventory:

• What is the style of the house? Is it traditional, modern or other? How will that affect your outdoor space?

• What materials were used in the construction of

the house? Is it made of wood, concrete, shingles? How will they affect materials for your outdoor space?

• Examine how one enters the house—is it the most appropriate means of entering the house? Is the walkway made of harmonious materials? Does it need to be enhanced or changed?

• Does one access the house from the street or from the driveway? What is the material of the driveway? Is it compatible with the house?

• How does the existing landscape relate to the geographic area? How does it relate to neighboring houses?

• From within the house, examine the views of the

Above: Build within the existing landscape. This well-placed gazebo or lookout blends seamlessly with the original tree-filled landscape.
Opposite: The sculpture serves as a focal point, situated on two axes perpendicular to one another. As such, it can be viewed from either the home or from the bench in the foreground.

Every problem has high style solutions. Take the problem and turn it into an accent. For example, in my own back-yard, I found myself surrounded and dwarfed by two-story homes on all sides. So I planted tall, deciduous trees. This did a few things: (1) it gave us privacy; (2) it created a wall along the back property line to landscape up to; (3) it created a canopy, or ceiling, as well as shade; and (4) it painted the back "wall" with color—through the seasonal changes in the color of the leaves. What was once the backside of my neighbor's house is now an integral part of our landscape master plan.

It is very important to ensure that all windows looking out to garden areas have great views. Walk through your home and consider your windows as picture frames and your landscape as a series of photographs.

property. Is there anything of interest framed through the existing windows and doors?

• Walk the perimeter of the property, and note the scale and size. Are there any particular areas that seem more suitable for a particular use?

• Are there any existing terraces, decks or exterior structures? Are they attractive and/or functional?

• Are there any extenuating environmental considerations? Excessive sun, rain or wind? Do you live near the ocean? In the desert?

• Notice the quality of light. Is there heavy shade? Partial or full sunlight? How does the light change with the seasons?

• Are there any areas of the property that are disagreeable? A view of a neighbor's garage, excessive traffic noise or power lines?

• Are there any particular strengths of the garden that would suggest a particular design direction? Focus on existing features, such as the house style, trees, ground levels and views.

DIY BASE PLANS

Unless you're a trained draftsman, producing an accurate base plan requires skills that are likely beyond your scope. For larger projects, it's best to understand each step of the designer's process so you can better assist, but leave the drafting to the designer.

If you're committed to doing it yourself, though, you can still follow the process and come up with a base plan like the one on page 30. Even for small projects like walkways or retaining walls, a base plan, with all the important dimensions and landscape elements recorded, is invaluable. It will help you later when it comes time to calculate quantities and purchase materials, and will also give you a much-needed perspective on the project. If the proposed space is out of

scale with the rest of the yard, for example, you may not notice that problem unless you have an aerial overview of it.

The tools you'll need are graph paper, tracing paper, a straight edge, a ruler and colored pencils. Any craft store should have these items. Your graph paper should have 1/4" squares if you're only doing the backyard and 1/8" squares if you're doing both front yard and backyard. You need to create a scale, and if you're using 1/4" ruled paper, the simplest one is making each 1/4" square = one square foot. Thus, 1" = 4 feet. (For 1/8" ruled paper, each 1/8" square = one square foot, and 1" = 8 feet.)

The first step is a freehand sketch to record all the important changes in

grade and existing dimensions. Measure the corner of the house to the beginning of the window. Measure all of the existing features on the house, including windows, doors, basement windows, downspouts, utility meters, faucets, electric outlets, air conditioners and exhaust from dryers. Mark all perimeter fencing, existing plant material, all existing hard materials and any existing features (sheds, pools). And make sure to check existing grades: Where is rainwater/runoff water going? That is often the most important thing we do.

Once you've recorded all the dimensions and other site features on your rough sketch, you're ready to transcribe them onto an accurate, scale drawing on your graph paper. Again, see page 30 for a good example.

Three. Analysis

At this point, the designer will put down a fresh piece of tracing paper on top of the base plan and start to mark off problems and solutions. If there are any existing problems or property issues that will affect your emerging design concept, now is the time to focus on them—and design around them. For example, if the neighbors have a shed you'd like to shield, you can try out different arrangements (fencing, walls, vine-covered lattice or even trees and/or shrubs) on the tracing paper. They'll hide the shed—and create a vertical element in your yard.

Plotting your site is actually the first formulation of the design because it will reveal project boundaries and limitations. By laying possible designs (in tracing paper) over the existing base plan, it will be clear whether the property can accommodate the number of separate spaces (i.e., terrace, gazebo, pool) you'd like to create, what size each space must be to serve its purpose and where the best sites are for each space. If you've done your inventory well, your base plan will allow you to

PHASED DESIGN

Budget and lifestyle can be factors in phasing design. Perhaps you can only afford to set aside a little bit each year for your landscape, or perhaps children create safety issues. There are two main principles to remember if you're phasing design:

1) Start from the back of your property and move forward. To avoid running over completed landscapes with heavy equipment, you should start from the furthest point from the street and move toward the street; you'll want to get the heaviest equipment in and out first.

2) Start with the hardscaping layout: To avoid re-doing softscape to make room for subsequent hardscaping projects, start with the hard elements.

Try to phase design in these stages:

A. Terraces, walkways & decks. These will give you living spaces to use immediately and will usually eliminate a later need for heavy equipment to be dragged through your garden.

B. Grading solutions. To ensure proper drainage and flow of rain and runoff water, retaining walls and/or drainage systems are top priorities.

C. Major waterscapes. If young children and safety are a concern, you may want to wait on this component; if budget is the main issue, though, you should prioritize your waterscape and wait to implement your front yard plans until you have the funds. Again, pools and waterfalls can require heavy equipment that may damage softscape.

D. Pergolas, arbors, trellises. Anything that's going to have posts and columns going down into the ground.

E. Tree plantings & sod. Put the big softscape in first; that's where you get the most impact. You get more mileage out of trees and lawn than you do out of shrubs. Your yard will look finished even if it's still a work in progress.

F. Shrubs & other plantings. It's far more cost-effective and easier to lay grass everywhere and then cut out the grass to replace with your shrubs.

During each of these steps, make sure to also consider irrigation and lighting systems for the garden. This reduces maintenance and ensures extended use of the garden into the evening hours.

assess whether the sites have good or bad views, whether they are private or exposed and other important considerations. Consequently, in this stage of design, you'll be able to develop effective individual solutions and designs that take maximum advantage of these issues. If these concerns are not clearly represented on the base plan, it becomes difficult to do a comprehensive analysis.

Four. Bubble Diagrams

With the analysis in hand, the designer will now draw a bubble diagram to illustrate what activities will take place within each area of the yard. The bubble diagram is produced on a fresh sheet of tracing paper that's overlaid on the inventory and analysis drawings in order to show both what currently exists and what could potentially be created. Even if creating a base plan is too

Think about connections between your home and garden spaces. Here, pathways lined with plants help frame the walkways that create the journey from one area to the next.

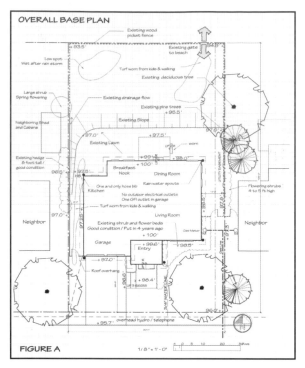

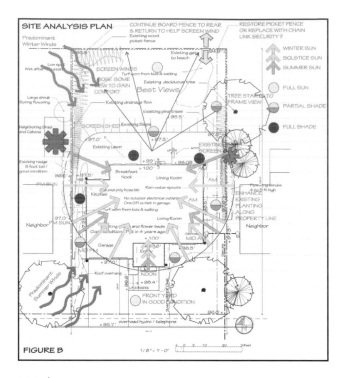

Site Inventory

Start with a careful inventory of the site, addressing these issues:

Wind: Wind direction varies with municipality, location and proximity to existing tall buildings, hills, mountains and lakes. Check with local meteorological service for direction, duration and typical strength of seasonal winds.

Precipitation: Check with local meteorological service for annual and monthly rainfall totals. (If you're hiring an irrigation contractor, he or she should have this information.)

Sun Exposure: Evaluate sun exposure, which will affect watering rates, plant material selection and your own comfort level. You can check the local library for books on calculating solar path angles. (A good resource is the American Institute of Architects' *Architectural Graphic Standards*, by Ramsey & Sleeper.)

Site Context: Evaluate neighboring trees, fences and buildings that can have a positive or negative effect on wind and sun exposure. Neighboring trees can hide unsightly views or block precious sunlight, while neighboring fences and buildings provide security but can also filter or block desired views.

Services & Utilities: Check with local service and utility companies for exact locations of underground utilities, such as telephone, gas, hydro-electric, cable TV and fiber-optic cables or pipes.

Easements & Right-of-Way Concerns: Check with local authorities for site easements for utilities or legal right-of-way issues.

Planning & Restrictive Covenants: Check your deed, title or purchase agreement for any restrictive covenants. Check with local authorities about property line setbacks, height restrictions and environmental regulations, especially with respect to drainage flows and volume. If you already have a survey plan, this will answer most of the basic questions, such as location of the house in relation to the property lines, fences and easements. Don't be afraid to call in a surveyor when there are questions of ownership, and never assume that fences are true property boundaries.

Wish List

Develop a wish list of design ideas and concerns you'd like to address in your outdoor space. Below is a sample that corresponds to the above drawings.

Large Entertaining Area: This area should be able to hold a table with six to eight chairs and still have room to maneuver. It should be sheltered from the wind, close to the BBQ and may need an umbrella or overhead lanai for shade. Screen from the kids' area.

Outdoor Shower: For beach excursions, it should be close to the gate. Check cost of running water line that far. Is a drain needed? (Check with authorities.)

Relaxation Area: This space should feel distant from more public areas, with some but not full sun so it doesn't get too hot. There should be room for a hammock or chaise lounge and wiring for outdoor speakers. (Check cost and electrical requirements for the latter.) A small water feature will add sound and block out noise.

Barbeque: Prefer a built-in unit, though unsure what type, so check local dealers, websites and magazines for ideas. Easy maintenance and clean-up is a must, and it should be close to the entertaining area. Check cost of running gas line, vs. using tanks. Since there will already be a water line for the shower, is a wet bar a possibility? It needs to be in area protected from full sun and not too close to the house—though close enough for kitchen runs. Countertop area? Storage space?

Kids' Play Area: This needs to visible from house and preferrably screened from the entertaining and relaxation areas. Swing set? Kit or custom built? Sources for kits? (Check with landscape architect or designer, and search manufacturers' websites.) Safety is an issue, so check with local authorities or landscape architects to see if they have guidelines. Do we need special surfacing given the amount of use it will get? Will kids prefer grass, sand, specialty play surfacing (i.e., rubber) or special sand/aggregate mixes?

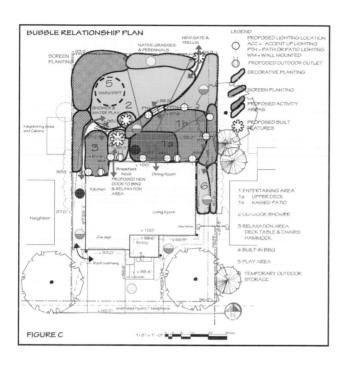

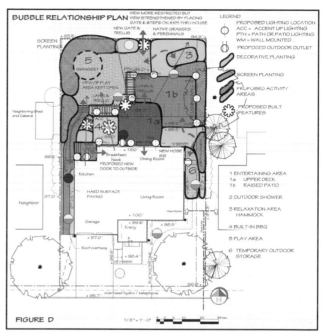

Expanded Wish List

As you start to create a bubble diagram, you'll encounter additional concerns, so continue expanding your wish list. The sample below addresses more practical issues.

Outdoor Lighting: Create lighting to extend hours of use into the evening, and put the system on dimmers to set moods. Make it visible from indoors to create interesting outdoor views. Ideally, security lighting turns on when we arrive home or go outside. Should it be set on timer(s), motion detectors or switches? (Check with electrician.)

Irrigation/Watering: Are there watering bans during the summer? (Check with authorities.) Any local ordinances on irrigation systems? Does it make a difference if we are on a well? Do we zone the property? Perhaps irrigation for native planting around the perimeter of the property, and none for xeriscape (drought-resistant plantings) around the house? Consult irrigation specialist.

Electrical Supply: Will we have to update our panel or put in an additional panel for outdoor requirements? (Check with local authorities for list of approved and accredited electricians.) What will the additional cost be to run outdoor electrical?

Outdoor Storage Area: Will we maintain the landscape ourselves? If yes, then we need a storage area or shed for mower, clippers, wheelbarrow, etc. Potting shed for annuals, splitting perennials? Space to store extra chairs and tables used when entertaining?

Security System: Check with local authorities to see whom they recommend. How easy is the system to use? What do neighbors use?

Budget/Phasing: Do we landscape the whole property? All at once? What do we do first? Front or back? How long are we staying here? How much value will this add to the house? (Check with real estate appraiser or agent, and look for comparisons in the neighborhood.) Based on the above, what are we really comfortable spending? How much is for improving our lifestyle, and how much is an investment?

Professional Design Development

Unless this is a small DIY project, you'll likely want to secure a professional team to fine-tune and execute your wish list. They can determine exact areas, initiate material selection and fully realize your ideas. Here are some issues to consider.

Purposes: This stage creates a basis for more accurate cost estimating and, by allowing for material changes based on those estimates, also facilitates "value engineering." Professionals will uncover any unforeseen problems, such as poor soil conditions or local restrictions, and may simplify the design to stay within budget.

What You Can Do to Prepare: If you've done your own basic drawings, you'll have something to help you select designers and contractors. Because you've already measured the site and developed basic concepts, a design professional can focus on fine-tuning the design to bring it up to industry standards. A good designer or builder will take your sketch, verify its accuracy and add their own ideas.

What to Do When Selecting Professionals: Always ask for references, always go view their past work and always talk to their past clients.

Working with a Landscape Architect or Designer: A landscape architect or designer will complete the design documents and work out construction details and a materials list. He or she will also develop construction documents that can serve as binding documents between you and your contractor. If you choose, they can also hire the contractor, oversee construction and even act as an arbitrator between you and the contractor in case of disputes.

Working in a "Design-Build" Relationship: The design-build contractor will also fine-tune your design, usually working with a landscape architect or designer on staff or retainer. They will take your sketch and prepare a ballpark budget. While their document preparation fees usually cost less than a landscape architect's, once you sign off on their bid, you are bound to them.

Working with a Contractor: If you're the only designer, make sure you're comfortable that the contractor understands your drawings.

You can establish different areas for entertaining by creating many rooms in your garden. As seen here, opposing elements like sun or shade, large or small, inclusive or secluded may all be incorporated in a single design.

One simple way of marking off prospective spaces is using twine attached to wooden stakes. Use the twine to mark each activity sphere, as well as paths of travel. This will help you visualize how the space will function and flow once it is built. Don't forget to see how the space looks from inside the house—the kitchen, the living room, or any places, such as an attic office, where you'll be admiring your garden. In addition to twine attached to stakes, you can lay out a garden hose to mark smaller areas.

daunting, you can and should play with bubble diagrams, using tracing paper to experiment with different layouts. Simply assign a bubble to every proposed space or activity. Common bubbles can be created for views, sun cycles and activities such as gathering (sitting areas), cooking (barbeques), eating (tables), sleeping/privacy (hammocks or secluded areas), playing (badminton, croquet or volleyball areas), swimming/bathing (pools or outdoor showers), comfort (chaise lounge chairs) and working (a shady place to turn on your laptop).

If you've decided you want to shield the view of your driveway from the terrace, you need to create a bubble (for shrubs, perhaps) to address that in this stage. Also, if you have certain spaces or activities that are important to you (e.g., sunbathing areas, a rock with a view of the sunset), they can be turned into bubbles as well, as can areas you'd like to illuminate at night, partition or otherwise distinguish. Ultimately, the bubble diagram will show a rough division of a property into functional living spaces that will help you see overlaps and transitions between spaces. Give every square foot a purpose, but don't worry about coming up with shapes yet. The focus at this stage is spatial layout and circulation. Remember that this process not only shows the positive spaces but also the negative spatial layout, or where there are holes in your design.

Five. Concept Design

When the bubble diagram has been completed and all the potential problems have been addressed, it's time to lay down another piece of tracing paper and start to sketch actual shapes that fit within your bubbles. This step requires a close look at circulation issues, so you'll need to address how one area flows into the next. How do you move between the barbeque, sitting area and furniture? Is there enough space? Or conversely, too much space? It's a good idea to take the master plan, go into the yard

and mark off the areas it describes to get a feel for scale and proportion, and to make sure that the spaces are comfortable in conjunction with the property and the house itself.

Concept design is an iterative process. Several designs should be created, and the best elements of each should be incorporated into one overall master plan. The concept design phase is also where tricky and somewhat subjective value judgments come into play. You're going

Don't forget to plan for secluded spaces. Here, a planting of fragrant roses makes this remote bench a quiet and inviting garden retreat.

You don't necessarily need to know all the plants that grow in your hardiness zone in order to be a good designer of plants. In fact, while I was in Los Angeles for a year studying environmental design, I began to work designing gardens. Because I didn't know the plant palette of the western United States, I was initially frustrated in my plant selections.

The owner of the nursery I was working with at the time reassured me that if I could imagine the shape, color and size of the tree or shrub I wanted to install, he would do the rest. Since he knew the plant palette, he was able to narrow down the possibilities to a few choices based on my descriptions of the types of plants I wanted to see.

I recommend the same to DIYers. Once you have an idea of size, shape and color, go to someone who knows plants in your area, like a nursery or a grower. They should be able to do the same as my old boss.

to need to make aesthetic choices and apply the fundamentals of design: the elements, principles and form composition. At this stage, the latter should be given the greatest weight. As the design becomes more developed, that's where the elements and principles come more into play.

Six. Detail Design

From this point on, a designer (you can do the same, of course) will create a series of detail drawings, each one further fleshing out the basic concepts for the space with structural notations for patios, gazebos, arbors and such, and notations for amenities that enhance and reinforce the theme you've chosen.

To establish an effective theme, start by taking a close look at the style or character of the house (i.e., Victorian, colonial, cottage, etc.) and the neighboring landscapes (i.e., wooded, waterfront, suburban). Based on your wish list and research into similar gardens, think about the style you wish to create in your outdoor space. Is what you wish to implement compatible with what exists? You may want to get a professional opinion on this. If it is not compatible, then decide how you can create a more seamless transition.

Planning for plantings is also an important part of this design stage. Most folks immediately start to worry about plants' zones of hardiness (you can find a map of North American hardiness zones at www.usna.usda.gov), as well as which plants do well in shade. Still, as seductive as those garden catalogs are, labeling actual plants is the last thing you should do. Your time is best spent focusing on the color, size, shape and seasonality of the plants that will work best with your design. If you want a tree, simply put a big circle in your detail design. Then you can talk to the nursery and describe what you want. Even if you just tell them you want a big mass of purple about waist high that lasts year-round, they should be able to point you toward the right plants.

Finally, you should start to address materials in this stage of design. Materials will be treated in more depth later in this chapter, as well as in the Material Quick Tours. For now, it's important to remember this principle: If money becomes an issue along the way, change materials, not the design. Do not ruin the integrity of the design to cater to a particular material; remember how much time and effort was spent on creating the master plan.

At this stage you should also incorporate lighting and irrigation systems, which will help you avoid maintenance hassles and get the most out of your design. An irrigation system, for instance, will keep your lawn looking healthy year-round, and night lighting will let you utilize your garden spaces

late into the night. Though these systems are not technically hardscaping, you should begin to think about them early in your planning, so that by the time you get to the construction drawing stage, you'll have already incorporated lighting and irrigation issues into your concept.

Lighting design will be dealt with more fully in Chapter 6, *Decorating Outdoors*. Here are some basic concepts to keep in mind for irrigation:

• *Address irrigation needs during the detail design phase*. Once you've decided on the core design and know where everything goes, you will have enough information to know where to place things.

God, they say, is in the details. Here, the introduction of sculpture adds visual beauty and doubles as an invitation for birds and other wildlife.

FOUR TYPES OF IRRIGATION

Drip Irrigation: This is a soaker hose that resembles a big piece of spaghetti with holes in it. There's no waste, and the plants adapt to it. Used in xeri-scape gardens (dry, arid climates).

Rotary Heads: Different heads for grass and planting beds. Grass requires a lot of water.

Pop-Up Heads: When it's time for irrigation, they pop out of the ground and rise 2" - 12" to water the surrounding area.

Manual: Even the good old-fashioned sprinkler can be programmed with a simple timer.

• *Irrigation systems are sunk below the hardscape.* Generally, you'll want to recess 3 1/2 " - 4" rigid PVC piping underneath your hardscaping (walkways, driveways and patios), which you can later use to pull your irrigation lines through. (You'll want to use a separate one for electrical lines.) Make sure that all isolated planting beds have piping leading to them so you can water them.

• *Double the codes.* Generally, I double the required size for PVC piping in case the site needs addi-

tional irrigation systems later—if, for example, the softscape expands.

• *Short watering intervals are best.* The ground has a saturation point, and once that's reached, the rest of the water rolls right off the top. It's far more effective to water your lawn for 15 minutes twice every other day than once for two hours. This is especially true when irrigating rooftop or balcony gardens. These types of planting beds will use a different, lightweight soil mixture that requires more water because of the adverse weather conditions.

• *The best time to water is in the early morning.* At 4 a.m., your irrigation system doesn't interfere with the house water. This ensures that water pressure is not lost through showers, toilets and washing machines.

• *Check that you have adequate water pressure in the house.* You can put a gauge on the water faucet to check pressure. You should have between 50 and 60 psi.

• *Check for volume of water.* You should have at least a 1" line coming into the house from the water company. If you have less than 1", you may need a booster pump to increase water pressure.

• *Understand the soil conditions you have to work with.* Sandy, well-drained soil requires more water, while clay soil requires less. Talk to somebody at your local nursery for more information on area soil needs.

• *Match your irrigation system to your needs.* Pop-up irrigation heads in planting areas with high shrubs will help you avoid the maintenance of irrigation heads mounted on bars or fences. (See sidebar.)

• *When irrigating a large garden area, consider installing a simple coupler as part of the system.* The coupler will allow you to quickly attach a garden hose to a water source when you are far away from the house faucet. By installing a quick coupler, you can easily attach a garden hose anywhere in the garden and wash down an area without storing lengths and lengths of hose.

If you're building architectural elements and water features, such as those in this backyard, don't proceed without a strong set of professional construction drawings. The building specifications of a hardscape are as important as the design itself.

Seven. Construction Drawings

The designer now must create an overlay of tracing paper that specifies all the requirements, materials and activities a professional crew will need to build your new spaces. (Of course, if you happen to be the crew, make sure that you understand how to read your designer's diagrams and that you can correctly interpret the construction drawings before accepting them.)

If this is an intensive landscape construction project, you should consult a professional to prepare a set of construction drawings. These drawings should consist of the following: 1) Layout plan, 2) Grading plan, 3) Planting plan, 4) Construction details (how to build the arbor, how to build the deck, how to build the retaining wall), 5) Lighting plan and 6) Irrigation plan.

There are some important reasons why you should commission construction drawings. Perhaps the most important is that they'll protect you from unforeseen cost-overruns: Together with the contractor's construction quote, these drawings are often a legal and binding contract for the owner. The drawings also give a contractor explicit instructions on how to build various aspects of the plan in detail, as well as where to source the materials for the project. Because of this detail, the construction drawings aid in cost estimating for the contractor and the homeowner. Construction drawings, in fact, are really an extension of design. Unless you take your proposed design out of plan view and put it into an elevation drawing, your contractor may not have a clear idea how to build something or whether it can be built at all.

Left: Properly planned spaces should integrate well with both the house and the surroundings. Here, hard materials help marry this home to the rural landscape. **Above:** Once you've got your final drawings, try again to visualize it from a variety of angles. This aerial view helps establish that all the hardscaping elements are properly proportioned.

Eight. Installation

Although most homeowners might not view this as a design step, it can often be the most critical one. There will be numerous decisions and changes you'll need to make due to issues that arise while your outdoor space is being constructed. For the DIYer, it may, in fact, be where you do most of your hands-on designing. No matter who does the actual implementation, plan out the sequence of construction events in the order they'll take place. This is an intuitive process, but you should follow the priorities of phased design. Here are some tips on how to make installation run smoothly:

• Once all the drawings are done, get at least three bids from reputable contractors. Remember: The lowest price does not always represent the best work.

• Check with your local landscape association to see if they have a contractor rating system in place. If so, ask for a report on the contractors who are bidding on your project.

• Ask to see a portfolio and letters of reference from each contractor. You should not only seek letters from the contractor's clients, but also from the landscape architects and designers he/she has worked with.

• Confirm that they are members of their local landscape construction association or belong to a professional association. Are they members in good standing of an appropriate workplace safety organization?

• Ask for proof of liability insurance. If they don't have it, you're liable for accidents on your property.

• Visit their completed projects where possible and talk with those clients.

• At this point, you can probably successfully choose a contractor.

• Establish a start date and a completion date. This will help minimize disruption in your household. Because of weather and difficulties getting material, these dates can be difficult to adhere to. If your job is large enough, you can insert a penalty clause, in which they might have to pay as much as 10% if they fail to complete the job by a certain date.

• Get written guarantees for all materials and workmanship for a minimum of one year. Some contractors will supply a two-year warranty.

• Establish terms of payment. Check with your local landscape association for acceptable terms.

• With the paperwork, the start date, the warranties

As these photos of an installation by landscape architects Bobbie Burdick and Jennifer Booher demonstrate, not every landscape project is for the do-it-yourselfer. The designers took a simple suburban fence and, with the aid of a good contractor, transformed this home's façade using boulders found in the landscape, concrete forms and a savvy design.

You don't want to design your dream project only to discover that building codes make much of it impossible to build, so make sure to look into local codes early in the process. You can find out what is feasible and what is not by contacting your municipal building department.

With no protection from the elements, durable stone, which needs virtually no maintenance, is a good choice of materials. This front walk has also been treated with a sealant to protect it from stains.

and payment terms, the job goes in the ground. Make sure you know how to maintain it. Contractors will not warranty mishaps caused by poor maintenance.

Nine. Maintenance

Maintenance issues are important cost considerations, and should, of course, be addressed in earlier planning stages. For each proposed design, you should ask your contractor or designer what the maintenance issues will be, so you won't have any surprises once your project is completed. Once it is complete, you'll then want to ask them to develop a four-season maintenance plan to help protect your investment. If you're doing it yourself, you should study your base plan and ask yourself the following questions:

- When do you fertilize and with what?
- When do you prune trees and shrubs? And what trees and shrubs do you prune?

- When and how do you cut dead branches from trees?
- How and when do you apply treatments for diseased plants?
- How do you clean and maintain paving surfaces?
- When do you silicone or apply a finish to hardscaping?
- How often should you paint or stain a deck or fence?
- At what height should you keep your grass cut?
- When should you aerate your lawn?
- What effects will air pollution have on your hardscape, and what are the remedies?
- Will you need to lift and re-lay any settled paving stones in your walkways or driveways?

Armed with your maintenance plan, base plan and construction drawings, you can now begin sourcing the best materials for the job.

Make sure to think of maintenance issues as you select materials. Colorful tiles can be a beautiful choice, but unless they are protected by a roof, as shown here, they can stain.

HARDSCAPING MATERIALS

Hardscaping materials are really the key to creating high style, low maintenance spaces, and picking the right material can make the difference in your outdoor garden rooms. To some degree, your design will dictate your choice of materials, as will your personal preferences and the availability of the materials you want.

When selecting materials, however, the largest consideration is making sure the materials are suited to the design as well as its proposed environment. If a particular material is too expensive, not durable enough for the application or unsuited to the climate, don't start compromising the design. Tempted to make room for a particular material in the budget, the schedule or the construction plans, you can end up compromising the larger vision. These types of compromises can create imbalances, such as one sumptuous corner in an outdoor living space with the rest seeming awkward or out of step.

For this reason, I defer materials selection until the

When choosing materials, think about complementing the house and property in every way.

latter stages of planning. Although you'll want to consider some basic ideas for materials as you go through the design process, I am a big advocate of keeping the integrity of the design intact and then, as needs or budget dictate, substituting different materials. If your first choice doesn't work out, it's fairly easy to find another material that will work just as well in the proposed design. This way, the integrity of the design remains intact even if you need to find a less expensive paver or a more readily available wood for the deck.

Sometimes materials can also answer site problems. One client, who badly wanted a second-story deck off the master bedroom, found that the railings mandated by building codes would all but obscure the view. In this case, installing glass panels as the deck railings left the view completely unobstructed and, at the same time, met code. Of course, when it rains—and frequently when it doesn't—the glass panels need to be washed, so be aware that there is often a trade-off between aesthetics and maintainability.

To get a sense of what materials you respond to best, the Materials Quick Tour in the following pages will give you a place to start the evaluation process. Above all, try to learn a little about each material you're considering well in advance of making the final decision. Pay attention to manufacturer statements about where and how their product is usually used—it may not be for lack of imagination that certain materials are always used for the same handful of applications. Once you gain an understanding of each material, the daunting array of possibilities will start to fall quite naturally into either the sensible or not-so-sensible category.

Designing with Materials

Some of it is common sense, some is "eye" and some is experience. Here are a few general precepts to keep in mind:

• *Never choose materials from samples on a showroom table.* Bring samples to the site. Do they blend in, harmonize, create a demarcation? As you approach, do they capture your attention or lead the eye out to the horizon? Does the cutting bed look small next to the boulders? Does the lacy wire fencing disappear into shadows from the forest? Also, make sure to check the materials at different times of day; materials look different in different types of light.

• *Sometimes two materials are better than one.* For example, flagstone looks great with interlocking stone, and the combination is cost-effective. Interlocking stone can be used with pebbles to create mosaics; weak materials can be used for structural applications if they're interspersed with stronger ones.

• *You don't have to use it as it comes, even if you want a totally natural effect.* For every material that doesn't have quite the right color, shape, texture or heft, there's a skilled craftsman who can make it so.

• *Synthetic materials are not necessarily bad for natural environments.* Some engineered materials are quite beautiful, as are some inspired combinations of synthetics and naturals.

• *Price has more to do with availability than performance.* The most expensive materials do not necessarily perform the best, while the least expensive materials can cost more to maintain year by year.

• *Consider size and shape before color or texture.* The former two are more powerful for setting a mood than the latter two.

• *Consider the architecture of the house.* A home is the centerpiece and largest element in any landscape, and the styles of both have to work together to achieve a pleasing and functional design.

• *Consider design and application.* Depending on usage, some materials may not be appropriate.

• *Consider surroundings.* Think not only about

1. *Everything relates back to the house,* including styles, materials and orientation. If your house says "colonial," your terrace shouldn't say "Bali."

2. *Garden destinations should never be treated as utilitarian.* They're little dream worlds that encourage the viewer to enjoy the natural surroundings. Try focusing on creating a destination that caters to the senses.

3. *The distances between garden rooms are transitions as well as conduits.* Traversing them should prepare a visitor to move from one experience to another. If your outdoor kitchen leads to a ridge where you can watch the sunset, leave the gleaming chrome behind.

4. *Make it classic.* Remember that the garden room is an extension of your home, and avoid the fads. You want people to ask "Has this always been here?" instead of "When did you do all this?"

immediate surroundings but also what's in the view. If your backyard spills into a wooded area, you'll want to choose materials that are congruous with the environment.

• *Treat each space as an extension of the one before it.* Think of each room, whether inside or out, as an extension of the one before it. In terms of materials, this means a certain consistency of scale, texture, and form.

Following Page: If you've designed structures and sought out materials that complement the architecture of the house, your hardscaping will, more often than not, flow seamlessly from indoors to out.

There are several things to consider with each material. Some issues are specific to the actual material (longevity, maintenance, appearance, color, texture and availability, for example), and some relate to the actual project (how the material will be used, how traffic patterns will affect it and how the material will work in combination with other materials, for instance). To aid in your selection, the Materials Quick Tours include capsule descriptions of common materials as well as pros and cons of each. As always, make sure to consult an expert for more detailed information.

CONCRETE & AGGREGATES

Concrete has come a long way from its sidewalk origins. Today, it's readily used throughout the landscape (walkways, stairs, driveways, walls, porticos, terraces and even furniture) and has earned its reputation as a strong, versatile material. It's predominantly made up of two components, paste and aggregates, with the paste—a mixture of water and Portland cement—serving as the binding agent, and the aggregate—a mixture of coarse and fine stone and sand—giving the concrete texture and strength. It's important to have both fine and coarse stones for strength, and water that is potable to eliminate impurities.

Concrete can easily be formed into any shape you can dream up, and because textures, colors and patterns can all be applied at the same time, it's truly inexpensive to customize. It has a long life span, is very rigid and is relatively tolerant to freeze/thaw cycles in regions where frost is an issue. However, the material's strengths, hardness and uniformity, are also potentially its drawbacks. It's not particularly cozy, and even in curved shapes it looks rather formal. Concrete can crack under extreme weather or pressure conditions but is generally maintenance-free and easy to repair.

1.

2.

3.

1. One way landscape designers make gray concrete look attractive is to surround it with colorful plantings. 2. The wet, or plastic, state of concrete allows it to take on virtually any shape. With the addition of color additives, gray tones can be replaced with softer hues.

3. The finished texture of concrete can range from a smooth trowel finish to a rough broom finish to a course stucco finish.

4.

5.

6.

Admixtures

The following admixtures can be added to your concrete to change its characteristics.

1. **Accelerator (calcium chloride):** This will help the concrete get stronger, quicker. This is great if you need to work right away with the concrete. With an accelerator, you can pull the forms (wooden braces that hold the concrete in place) away much sooner.

2. **Retarder (starch, acid or cellulose):** This admixture slows the curing process and maintains the concrete in its concrete form for an extended time. If you're trying to apply a certain finish to the concrete and you've got a large surface area to finish, a retarder will keep the concrete from hardening to keep your finish consistent.

3. **Air - entrainment (sulfonated compounds, fats, wood resins):** These substances cause air bubbles to form, which is important when you're pouring concrete outside. Air increases the resistance to freezing and reduces the weight of the concrete. Any type of exterior concrete in freezing climates needs to have "concrete with air."

4. **Coloring agents:** Powder or liquid pigment that's added to the concrete to change its color. Gives you a unique surface finish.

Architectural Concrete

As it is termed today, this material may be colored, stamped or patterned. Concrete finishes include:

• **Colored concrete:** In addition to mixing colors in, you can paint the dried surface, although I caution against this. It doesn't have a chance to fully integrate in the concrete as it sits and can peel or wear off later. To avoid maintenance issues, mix the color in with the concrete when it is wet. That way the color has the chance to fully become part of the concrete. This will reduce further maintenance.

4. With the use of molds and admixtures, concrete can be made to look like virtually any stone. Authentic textures and jointing, combined with the low comparative cost of installation, make this material a popular choice. **5.** Designs can be interwoven to create very unique products. Silicone finishes, available in matte, semi- gloss or gloss finish, help protect the concrete surface. **6.** Through the use of admixtures, the concrete cures at different rates, which allows time to create highly detailed images or logos. Here, the final coloring has been added prior to the template being removed.

- **Hand Troweling:** Smooth finish, done by hand. This can be slippery when wet.
- **Broom Finish:** Taking a bristle broom and dragging it across in lines. It creates the gritty look familiar in most sidewalks and gives you traction in snow or rain.
- **Stucco or Stipling Finish:** With the concrete surface freshly laid, the contractor will use a device that essentially spits small droplets of cement onto the surface to give it the stucco look.
- **Patterned Concrete:** Salt or sand can be sprinkled onto the concrete, a broom may be brushed across wet concrete to create patterns or water may be blasted across the top.
- **Stamped Concrete:** This finishing technique entails stamping moulds, such as cobbles, into wet concrete. Stamped or patterned concrete requires real craftsmanship, so make sure you have the right contractor for this job.
- **Exposed Aggregate Concrete:** This finish, which leaves small pebbles exposed on the surface, is widely used today, largely because it's so easy for the client to select the size, shape and color of the pebble. Done right, exposed aggregate concrete can resemble luxe materials like terrazzo or be color-matched to a brick or stucco residence.

When installing exposed aggregate concrete, many people will pour the concrete base, seed the pea gravel (pebbles) on the surface and then tamp it down to embed it in the concrete. This method will look right when done—it just won't last. By tamping the concrete, you're creating air bubbles, that will allow moisture in; when the moisture freezes, it will pop the pea gravel out. The better method is to add the pea gravel when you're mixing the concrete and then spray the wet surface to expose the aggregate.

1.

2.

3.

1. Landscape architect Michael Schneider creates beautiful mosaics by selecting materials such as stone, glass or metal, and pressing them into the wet concrete mix after it has been poured. (It's fine to tamp the aggregates into the concrete in decorative applications such as this.) **2.** Exposed aggregate finishes, seen here with local pea gravel and wood dividers, are popular surfaces for poured concrete. You can select varying textures, from very rough to very smooth, for your finish. **3.** Exposed aggregate finishes come in many colors and types. Be sure to select an aggregate that complements the exterior of the house.

Pouring Your Own Concrete

1 part cement, 2 parts sand, 3 parts gravel (or aggregate), 6 parts water. When it's poured, it's still very plastic. To achieve maximum strength, it must sit undisturbed for approximately 28 days. Concrete continuously cures. It gets harder as every day goes by. If you're using it as a base for another material (i.e., mortar), you can work with it the next day. If used as a finish (i.e., as a driveway), it's wise to let concrete harden for a good week.

PROS:

1. Long life span. Installed properly, it can last virtually forever.
2. It's universally available.
3. It comes in a variety of colors and finishes.
4. Because of its plasticity, it can be formed into any shape you can dream up.
5. Versatile in weight; because you can add air, you can make it lighter.

CONS:

1. You can install it only when the weather's above freezing.
2. If it stains or cracks, you can't replace segments or pieces. You have to replace the whole thing to achieve a uniform look.
3. You can't install large areas in one piece. Maximum pours for concrete are 400 square feet; anything larger and you need to put in control joints and expansion joints to allow for shifting and cracking.
4. You have to reinforce concrete with steel and mesh.
5. It requires time to set. Once you've poured it, you've got to wait before you can actually use it.

4.

5.

6.

4. Stamped concrete patios are common pool deck material. It is important to select a finish that will be easy on bare feet and won't be slippery when wet. 5. You can impress moulds, with lettering, designs or both, when concrete is in its wet, or plastic, state.

6. Stamped and colored concrete can be poured and dry in one day. Should there be any shifting or settlement over a harsh winter, the whole slab will move together and settle back into position as one piece. This reduces future maintenance.

Patio Slabs

Another form of concrete is the pre-cast patio slab, which is traditionally a developer's favored material for walkways and patios, largely because it is inexpensive to purchase and install. Unfortunately, since there is not a lot of selection and variation for patio slabs, an area paved with this material can be monotonous in appearance. Because slabs are large and thin, the chances of cracking are great, and they will also teeter if the surface is not absolutely level beneath them. Normally, developers use this is as a temporary walkway or patio to get permits.

ASPHALT

Asphalt at one time was nearly synonymous with driveways for two reasons: It's fairly inexpensive to supply and install, and its dark color absorbs heat and helps to melt snow faster than any other material. Although in residential projects it's still used mainly for driveways, asphalt can also be a good choice for walkways, tennis courts and the base for large ponds. It is one of the most inexpensive hardscaping materials, and the availability of colored and stamped asphalts has made this material more widely used. It is possible to achieve many of the same decorative finishes as stamped and colored concrete for as little as half the price. Some impressed and patterned asphalts nicely reproduce the texture and look of natural and interlocking stone without feeling flimsy. (Please see the section on "Interlocking Stone" in *Materials Quick Tour 2*.)

1.

2.

3.

1. Large concrete slabs can be purchased, or made, to suit any condition. When inter-planted with ground cover or pea gravel, you have a low maintenance solution for a secondary or tertiary walkway. **2.** Creating an exposed aggregate driveway with a smooth concrete-finish soldier course is a creative alternative to asphalt.

3. Driveways should be considered part of the landscape. Here, a sand-textured concrete driveway is used in conjunction with a darker soldier course.

4.

Laying Asphalt

Asphalt gets its strengths in layers, so make sure your contractor installs your asphalt driveway in two layers. First, install a 2" base layer of asphalt containing coarse aggregates, followed by a 1" top layer containing fine aggregates. Also, be wary of the contractor who promises he can do this for much less than his competitors. Some unscrupulous contractors may pour less asphalt in the middle. So be home when the asphalt is poured, and make sure they're not filling the middle of your driveway with a mound of gravel.

PROS:

1. It's inexpensive.
2. You can do this in large areas with no joints.
3. Absorbs heat to melt snow.
4. You can use it soon after installation.
5. It's easy to patch. You can get asphalt in bags from the hardware store to replace stained or cracked sections.

CONS:

1. If asphalt doesn't get a lot of use, it can dry and crack.
2. Unlike concrete, which may not require an aggregate base, asphalt needs a very solid, compacted gravel base. A driveway should be excavated up to 18", with up to 15" of compacted gravel.
3. Because of heat absorption, it can scar or disfigure on a hot day. Something as simple as a bike kickstand, for instance, can leave an impression in hot asphalt.
4. Asphalt and gasoline don't mix. If you have a leaky car, it willl eat the surface of the asphalt.
5. Snowplows can tear or even roll up the surface of the asphalt.

4. Asphalt is commonly used for roads and driveways and tends to be popular for its unique heating and cooling properties. Despite its less than optimal color, the black tar finish is practical because it absorbs heat on warm summer days and helps melt snow during cold, icy winters.

CHAPTER 2

ROOMS WITH A VIEW
PORCHES, TERRACES & DECKS

A porch, a terrace or a deck can give you what your house can't—space to host dinner for 20 under the moonlight or space to sit with your laptop and watch the sunset. Unlike garden rooms that usually require a

stroll down a flower-lined path, these are transitional spaces most often attached to the house, and you can enjoy them in your slippers should you choose to.

Just how important are these areas that, unique among our landscaping elements, serve as both transitional and living spaces? My wife and I recently bought a house that was beautiful in all respects save one: There was no front porch. It didn't seem a big issue until we moved in and discovered that we felt deprived of an outdoor living space that connected us to our neighborhood. Our solution was to create a front courtyard, which we did by enclosing an area between the driveway and the front door. A low stone wall at seating height creates the bottom section of the partition, while a cedar lattice and pergola complete the top section and overhead. With trees, flowering shrubs and vines growing in front of and on the woodwork, a wonderful scene is set with areas of sun, shade and shadow. You have the option to see out but not be seen or to sit in view of the passing traffic.

It made a big difference. This new area allows us to watch the children play, get out of or into the shade, communicate with our neighborhood, or simply eat, drink and doze. Consequently, the amount of time we spend outside has increased substantially, as have our friendships with the people on our block.

So what is the best way to live outdoors? We should begin with a discussion of what might best be called proper outdoor rooms—porches, terraces and decks. These types of outdoor spaces are often the centerpieces of our landscape and serve many of the same purposes as interior rooms.

Opposite: Exterior dining on a porch, terrace or deck can create a comfortable atmosphere unmatched by even the finest indoor dining room. **Above:** Defining an exterior dining room with a hard edge, such as a stone wall and architectural screening, helps create a comfortable setting for a romantic dinner for two or dinner party for ten.

The Five S's

Every design choice comes with pros and cons, and the only way to make the appropriate decision is to assess both the architectural style of your house and your lifestyle needs. Here are some helpful ways to think about designing your core garden rooms. I call them the Five S's:

1. Seclusion: Adequate privacy is important. A sense of seclusion can be achieved in a porch, deck or terrace with proper architectural screening and plantings. In an urban setting or rooftop garden, screening is critical. As anyone raised in the country knows, even a screen door can be a polite form of privacy if you want it to be.

2. Sequencing: Sequencing refers to how a porch or terrace functions within the house's greater circulation plan. Do you plan to use the porch simply as part of an entry sequence (i.e., welcoming guests by the front door), or do you foresee creating living space by adding a swing? Is the terrace meant to double as an entrance to a garden walkway? When evaluating sequencing, make sure to consider the space's functionality in all four seasons. As you visualize entry sequences for your porch, for example, think about whether a bench near the front door would be a good place to take off snow boots in the winter.

3. Shelter: In inclement weather, a simple roof can be invaluable, as it gives you time to shake the water off your umbrella and dig in your pockets for house keys. If you're opting for an uncovered terrace, make sure the main entrance from the house is well sheltered. The most basic kind of shelter is a portico, which can be found on houses of almost every architectural style—from Mediterranean to modern, Carpenter Gothic to colonial revival. Porticos do not have to be fancy. They are shelter in its simplest terms—a roof, perhaps supported by corbels and arches, perhaps sided with benches and columns, but most definitely defined by its overhead structure.

4. Style: Formal or informal, your garden room has to match the style and architecture of your house. A sleek deck looks like an afterthought on a traditional house. A rustic stone terrace billowing with plantings looks out of place on a strictly formal colonial home.

5. Surroundings: Your outdoor room is not an island. Just as it has to be integrated into the architecture of your house, it also has to suit the rest of your garden and indeed the rest of your neighborhood. If your porch, deck or terrace is on the front of a suburban home, the design of the rest of the houses on the street should be taken into account.

Sequencing, shelter and seclusion make this a great garden setting. The transition from the steps to the patio makes you feel as if you have entered a gateway into another space. The overhead trellis creates a cozy atmosphere and casts wonderful architectural lines.

The formal style of this terrace echoes the symmetry of the house architecture. The two spaces work in harmony and seem like one cohesive thought.

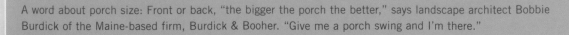
A word about porch size: Front or back, "the bigger the porch the better," says landscape architect Bobbie Burdick of the Maine-based firm, Burdick & Booher. "Give me a porch swing and I'm there."

PORCHES

A porch is the closest thing to an actual room you can create outside. Fitted with screens, it can provide protection against marauding mosquitoes and other pests. And because it is far more weatherproof than a deck or terrace, it can be decorated like an indoor room, with draped tables and cushions covered by beautiful fabrics, or with a rug for comfort under foot and a ceiling fan to lure the breezes. In winter, screens can be swapped for storm windows and the porch converted to a very pleasant sunroom.

Usually built at the same time as the house, the porch is generally the purview of the architect. In fact, if your home doesn't have a porch, I recommend consulting one familiar with your house's style prior to building any extensions to your home. For landscaping elements separated from the home, there's a bit more margin for error in terms of integrating with the house. With a porch, you have to make sure your materials, styles, structures and other architectural elements are extensions of the existing structure. Front or back, you don't want to create a clash of styles.

Keep in mind that the addition of a porch will also affect interior rooms by making them both darker and cooler. Porches serve as a form of insulation, buffering a house from heat and allowing breezes to circulate. Southerners have long been so fond of porches that they've added second-story screened outposts to draw breezes onto the bedroom floor. In summer months, these become sleeping porches, sheer heaven for children and adults alike.

Usage is also an important consideration. Is this a sitting porch? A dining porch? A simple entry sequence? As you design it, make sure that you're taking into account all the appropriate uses for the porch. The most common one is providing shelter for the front door. When towns were small and suburbs less dependant on automobiles (and televisions), the sheltering front porch was a place where neighbors sat and caught up on life and news. Today, however, privacy is more of a concern and front porches are often an unused space. If that's an issue, try incorporating simple trellises, fences or other subtle forms of enclosure so you can use the space for more than an entry sequence.

Back porches have the obvious advantage of being more secluded and private than front porches. Often raised above the garden to protect against the effects of moisture, the back porch needs to be clearly integrated into the hardscape design. All of your outdoor built environments need to relate to the house, and you should view the back porch as the most direct link to the landscape. To accomplish this, many people build a terrace right off the back porch to create a transitional space— and a more expansive place to host dinners.

However you integrate the porch into the outdoors, be sure to think of how it can serve as both transitional and living space. Even if you envision a porch that is simply a place to wipe off your muddy boots, a small touch such as a bench can turn it into a place to catch your breath and watch the sunset.

This porch area would make anyone feel right at home outdoors. The value of the porch is increased because it has multiple uses, serving as a dining area, a reading space and a family den.

Even a simple porch entry can be very attractive. More than just a shelter for the front door, this porch, with a simple chair and welcoming steps that can double as seating, harks back to the days when the front porch was used to greet neighbors and passers-by.

Above: The size of a terrace should relate to the size of the house and property. Scale and proportion should be carefully considered when laying spaces that are both visually appealing and physically comfortable.
Opposite: Consistency is key. The modular layout of the natural flagstone gives the terrace a formal feeling repeated in the furniture arrangement.

DESIGN TIP

A good rule of thumb: In a small garden, it is important that the area devoted to the terrace should be larger than the area devoted to the plantings. This ensures that the living space (the terrace) and the decorative space (the garden) are properly proportioned. You don't want to feel surrounded by your plants!

TERRACES

Every garden room needs a floor, and a terrace supplies that with a variety of sturdy materials. Blue stone, flagstone, concrete, brick, grass and many of the materials mentioned in the Materials Quick Tour sections can be used effectively for terraces. Keep in mind, however, that any guest appearing with high heels will be grateful for a flat, even surface. As a host, you'll also be happy for the stability when you serve dinner and don't have to squeeze little matchbooks under table legs.

What size should your terrace be? If you're planning to host large dinners, it needs to be at least the size of your dining room. Twelve by twelve is a good starting point, but what's spacious indoors can feel paltry outdoors. "Getting the proportions right is tricky," says Bobbie Burdick. "Our rule of thumb is that the length of a terrace should be two-thirds the building's height. We measure the façade, and if it's a two-story house and 24 feet tall, then we'll make the terrace a good 15 to 20 feet. You know when the dimensions are incorrect. When they're correct, the terrace just feels soothing."

Some of Burdick's clients want terraces large enough to host cocktails for 50. In that case, she'll break the shape up and add plantings in the middle. Even a modest-sized terrace can benefit from a few flagstones being removed and herbs, flowers, ground cover, grass or even trees planted in their place.

Terraces can be strict squares or rectangles defined by plantings or low walls that double as seats. Or they can be organic, irregular shapes that almost bleed into the garden, perhaps with paving stones that become more widely spaced at the edges and are intermingled with flowers and herbs. Whatever style terrace you choose, it is critical that its design be compatible with your house's architecture. In fact, it's more important that the shape of your terrace integrate with the shape of the house than the yard.

Siting also is important. When deciding where to place the terrace, here are some key issues to keep in mind:

Breezes: Especially for windy areas like waterfront properties, you'll want to have a good idea how breezes affect your terrace.

Sun cycles: What's the morning light like on your property? The evening light? Is there a good shade tree that will shield the glare of the afternoon sun?

Views: The terrace is often the centerpiece of your landscape, and you'll likely want to site your terrace to accentuate the best view you have.

Screening: Likewise, you can site the terrace (and any enclosure you're designing with it) to shield yourself from any views you wish to avoid.

Proximity to the house: If you plan to entertain, you may want your terrace to lead easily to the kitchen, for example.

Grading: Would a retaining wall allow you to turn the sloping backyard into usable space? A terrace can often be a grading solution when the ground slope is too steep.

Flooring for Terraces

Make sure to choose the right flooring for your terrace. Patterns and texture can add interest to any terrace, with the center, perhaps, a brick circle and the areas surrounding it laid with concrete pavers or flagstone. A good place

BASIC TYPES OF
FLOORING FOR TERRACES

1. Gravel: Beautiful, but because it requires regular maintenance, it's not optimal for frequently used terraces.

2. Ceramic Tiles: Though expensive and easily stained, they create an immediate and often stunning presence.

3. Unglazed Tiles: With a more natural look than ceramic tiles, they can take stains and still have a beautiful patina.

4. Concrete: Utilitarian and, contrary to popular conceptions, it can be finished to have the look of high design.

5. Brick: Integrates well with more traditional homes.

6. Stone: Creates a natural look, especially if placed randomly.

7. Pre-Cast Stone: Can be tailored to precisely fit a wide variety of needs.

8. Natural: If distinguished from the yard by an edging material, well-kept grass can be all the flooring needed for a terrace.

From top to bottom: (1) Gravel can be used in areas of the garden that show great detail in planting or architecture. (2) Random flagstone spilling onto a natural terrace helps create a transition in this garden setting. (3) Plants in the joints of flagstones help soften the appearance of a large stone mass. (4) Pavers set at 45-degree angles enlarge space.

Consider repetition of materials to help add character to your terrace. Here, the seating wall in the foreground matches the house brick, and the flagstone on the terrace floor is extended to the pool area.

The non-textured concrete stone terrace matches the clean,
non-textured surfaces of the house and columns, while the terrace's
modular flagstone echoes the jagged stone on the façade.

Top: Curved stairs within a modular flagstone terrace can act as a wonderful transition from one area to another, serving as a dramatic entryway. **Bottom:** Random flagstone pieces, large and small, are the perfect complement to a natural setting. Becoming one with your surroundings is an important factor when designing your terrace.

to start is by taking a close look at the adjacent interior room. You can marry the terrace with your living space, for example, by continuing the tile or terra cotta that's in the room. (Keep in mind, however, that outdoor ceramic tile is large and thicker than indoor tile.) Naturally, this isn't as much of a concern for terraces that are separated from the house by a walkway, but, as with all components of your hardscaping, you should make sure you match the style of the terrace flooring with the style of the house.

You also need to think through the uses for your terrace. If you're planning to do a lot of cooking, unglazed patio and quarry tile, available with a nonskid surface for safety, are attractive and easy-to-clean choices for barbecue areas. (One caveat: Tile needs to be laid on a perfectly flat surface.) On the other hand, a nicely colored pea gravel terrace may look great but could become a maintenance headache if you plan to entertain. Unless protected with a sealant, stone or brick may discolor if you spill things on them.

Cooking Outdoors

If one of the goals of creating an outdoor room is dining, you're probably going to want a grill. If this were the 1950s, you'd be advised to build a brick barbecue pit. Today, grilling is often a much more serious affair, with grills (and sometimes warming ovens and refrigerators) designed into the hardscape of terraces, either in walls or their own special unit. Sometimes grilling areas are given a roofed space so that cooks can be sheltered from the rain, a feature that assures the units will be used regularly. Sometimes they have built-in tables; sometimes they count on walls to hold grilling utensils and platters.

Today's grills can be elaborate and expensive, or simple Webers wheeled to a spot by the kitchen door. Whichever type of grill you choose, you should consider where you'll want to cook when you start planning the design of your terrace, porch or deck. "A barbecue has got to be situated in a place where it's going to be accessible but also where it's safe for kids and for traffic patterns," says Jay Archer, a landscape designer and president of John Jay Landscape Management in Katonah, New York. "You have to have a comfort level of getting from the kitchen to the barbecue and to where you're serving your guests. You also don't want the smoke to rise and stain any part of the house or cause a fire threat." And if you don't want to be a lone chef, flipping your salmon in solitude, you'll want the grill situated near chairs so guests can pull up a seat and chat (or better yet, help with the cooking.)

Opposite: A change in the ground plane (i.e., flagstone to brick) can help define garden rooms without the use of walls or other forms of separation. **Right:** Innovative solutions to outdoor cooking, such as modern stainless steel units, are replacing mobile units and can be mounted virtually anywhere.

SHELTER
WITHOUT A ROOF

On a terrace or deck, enclosure overhead is important. Umbrellas and retractable or louvered awnings can provide intimacy and sun protection. Vine-covered pergolas (see Chapter 3, *Enclosure*) are a romantic option.

The most common form of shelter is the market umbrella. Its shape and color should be carefully considered because it will certainly be a focal point when viewing your terrace from the far corners of your garden. Green is a common choice because it blends in with trees and shrubs. However, green umbrellas cast unflattering shadows on guests and food. Yellow, on the other hand, gives tables a Tuscan glow. Off-white is an attractive choice, especially if a terrace or deck is surrounded by gardens with pastel hues.

The best umbrellas are wind-proof and designed to tilt for constant sun protection. Some have wheels so they can be moved as the light shifts. In lieu of a bulky metal base, umbrellas can be set directly in a terrace in specially designed holders.

1. Be aware of gutters and drip lines to avoid the nuisance of dripping water from the house.
2. Pay attention to the shadow of the house, particularly if it's a very large house; your terrace or deck will be at its mercy.
3. If you're planting trees, position them far enough from a terrace to avoid the buckling created by large roots. Choose trees that don't shed messy berries, seeds or sap.
4. If the terrace abuts a house, it needs to be a step down for weatherproofing. Similarly, a deck needs to be a step down if there's a chance of accumulated snow.
5. Outmoded concrete terraces can be resurfaced, enlarged or linked to a new terrace with the addition of brick or flagstone.
6. Don't overlook the possibility of decks, porches and terraces in a side yard. A secluded spot off a bedroom, library or office can be the perfect spot for an outdoor room.
7. Once you have a terrace or deck, you'll want to admire it from inside the house. Add French doors or extra windows to enhance the view.
8. The architect's rule of thumb for determining the size for a porch, terrace or deck: When in doubt, make it larger.

Building a Terrace

Since a terrace is a large surface that has to be stable and flat, installation really matters. (You don't want to have to keep a box of wedges handy for straightening out wobbly tables.) Think about whether the hardscaping will be laid on soil, gravel or concrete. Laying harder elements on soil is not recommended, especially in regions with cold or wet seasons. The ground will heave sooner or later and, come spring, your terrace may have waves in it.

The preferred solution is to excavate the area and replace the topsoil with granular material, such as crushed stone or sand, that can be compacted completely. The hardscaping is then laid on top of this foundation. In some areas, bricks, granite sets, flagstone or natural stone can sometimes be mortared on top of a concrete slab. Ultimately, this is one of the best forms of installation; should anything move over the course of the winter, it will all shift and settle together, preventing any localized upheavals.

Above: As you design outdoor rooms, make sure to leave adequate room for circulation around site furniture, especially the type you'll want to move with the sun. **Opposite:** Here, the colors and textures of the house are carried into the design of the terrace, creating harmony between the outdoor space and the façade of the house.

Decks and architectural carpentry features should first and foremost complement the existing architecture of the house, including the building shape and material.

DECKS

A ubiquitous suburban feature, decks have acquired something of a tarnished reputation, often because little creativity goes into their design. But a deck can be an extraordinary asset to a house, especially when it captures an amazing view or is cantilevered (anchored into the house, without the benefit of columns to hold it up) over a hillside, literally borrowing entertaining space out of thin air. A deck can provide a level surface on an awkward lot and is an excellent way to cover up a boring old concrete patio.

Unlike stone, a wooden deck stays cool in the heat of the day, making it a good play place for children. Design it around existing trees (or leave pockets for new trees to grow up), and a deck can be an extremely satisfying outdoor room. If trees are a priority, a deck is a good choice because the post system is much less likely to damage the roots of trees than the laying of a terrace. Because of the gaps between the boards, decks eliminate excavation and drainage problems associated with terraces. (The gaps, however, do have a downside: They

tend to snare high heels. If you plan on formal entertaining, keep that in mind.)

One reason decks have acquired a tarnished reputation is that many are applied without any concern for a house's architecture. "Stick a deck on a Cape and it looks silly," maintains Burdick. "I think decks on most older homes look silly." A deck that is integrated into neither house nor garden is a forlorn space that is not likely to be used. There's nothing worse than eating dinner, suspended in the middle of a neighborhood, high above the shrub line that shelters conventional terraces.

On the other hand, with a little thought, decks can be turned into private oases. If you live close to your neighbors, it just takes a little more planning. You can grow vines on a trellis wall or plant a virtual hedge in raised planters. You can even add a small fountain for noise protection. To create this type of space, simply think of the deck as another garden room. Where you build entrances and exits, how you guard against the neighborhood noise and what type of enclosure you design for the deck will help determine its level of seclusion. (For more ideas on

Wood decks are a good alternative to stone decks around a pool, helping to warm up the garden room and make it inviting.

Top: Wood decks can act as the perfect garden transition. As the cedar weathers, it turns to a subtle gray, which complements its surroundings.
Bottom: Rooftop gardens and container gardening are becoming more popular. Simple rubber-lined planters help make this urban space a livable outdoor garden room.

maintaining privacy, see Chapter 3, *Enclosure*.)

There are many ways to make the actual style of a deck distinctive. Flooring can be planned so that the diagonal slant of the boards makes the space dramatic. Pinwheels, checkerboards and herringbone patterns can also enhance the look of a deck, while railings can double as benches and/or flower boxes. Or railings may be treated more like fences, painted white and designed in any number of traditional patterns and finished with finials and decorative details.

Finally, think of ways to integrate your deck with the garden. Decks create a wonderful staging area for you to experiment with all sorts of container gardens. You can plant herbs, cultivate a hummingbird garden, lure butterflies, sculpt topiaries, and brighten cold spring mornings with bulb gardens. Filling your deck with plants is one of the best ways to link it to the garden and make it a welcoming transition space.

ROOFTOP AND BALCONY GARDENS

The new frontier in porches and terraces is rooftop and balcony gardening. For apartment dwellers, these areas can create valuable outdoor space. Think of all of the empty roof spaces available for greening the environment in any given city. Imagine an avenue whose upper reaches are lined by gardens and terraces instead of the usual welter of cables, antennas and poles. Such spaces are still rare, but they give back tenfold in terms of air quality and quality of life. The beneficiaries of an urban terrace are not just the homeowners and their guests but also thousands of passersby.

The major factor in designing a balcony or roof garden is the sheer weight of the hardscaping and plant material used. If you're undertaking a rooftop installation, this is likely not a DIY project unless you happen to be a structural engineer. (Or a botanist, for that matter: High above the ground, wind and sun exposure intensify,

1. *Make it comfortable for everyday use as well as for entertaining.* Your outdoor room needs to hold whatever size group you plan to entertain and also feel intimate when it's just you and your morning coffee. A series of small tables might work better than one large one. Think too about storing most of your seating inside the house. Just make sure you have a comfortable chair ready for each member of your family.

2. *Make it functional.* Your outdoor room has to serve a lifestyle purpose. It has to be more than a mudroom or a dropping off point for sports equipment. What will make it work is furniture that functions, access to the house and garden and adequate privacy.

3. *Make it stylistically appropriate.* A porch, deck or terrace should not be an architectural afterthought. It is a transitional space between house and garden and needs to be integrated with both.

4. *Make it spacious.* Though you can have a terrace or porch that's too big and clunky, it's much harder to overdo than to underdo. Chances are, you're going to love your outdoor room so much, you'll want it to be spacious. So don't scrimp in the planning stages.

and only a limited variety of plants can withstand them.) When designing a balcony or rooftop garden, the best resource is a seasoned professional who will help you navigate building codes, structural issues and important landscaping concerns.

TILE & BRICK

Tile and brick are popular choices for walls and ground surfaces. Best used in a mild climate, both brick and tile should be prepared at a higher temperature (highly fired) for outdoor purposes and colder climates. To tell a highly fired brick or tile from one that isn't, take two bricks off the palette and clang them together. If you don't hear a ringing sound, they have likely been fired at a lower temperature and should be discarded.

The sheer expense of installing tile and brick has convinced many people to opt instead for interlocking stone. At a fraction of the price, it provides similar geometry, looks good and is far easier to maintain (see below). If cost is not a concern, however, there will always be good reasons to use ceramic tiles or clay brick pavers. Certain historical house genres—older Victorians, vernacular colonials, Gothics—simply look best surrounded by period materials. Ceramic tiles are also a spectacular way to tie outdoor and indoor rooms together. Simply extend the flooring of a solarium or kitchen right through a set of glass doors and onto an adjacent patio.

PROS:

1. They're very rich in color and possess an inherent beauty.
2. Because they're fired at a high temperature, they have a high compressive strength and can bear a great deal of weight.
3. Because they are so dense, they resist disfigurement and abrasion.
4. Traditionally, they come only in modular shapes, which makes them easy to install.
5. They integrate with certain types of homes exceptionally well.

CONS:

1. They're among the most expensive pavers.
2. They're susceptible to salt damage, so in snowy climates make sure to use only sand for traction.
3. Quality control is an issue: You need to check each brick to eliminate poorly fired ones.
4. Visually, they work best with specific styles of homes.
5. From an installation standpoint, making curves is difficult.

1.

2.

3.

4.

1. Numerous colors and grades are available when selecting tile. Make sure to consider its intended use. Often that will dictate the grade, which in turn will dictate available colors. **2.** Tiles should be chosen by quality and color to complement the architecture of the house. Today, the wide variety of color options makes buying tiles a much easier and more interesting task. **3.** Combining bricks and flagstone is a winning solution to any hardscaping dilemma. **4.** The richness inherent in clay brick pavers makes them a natural choice for residential use. They accentuate the landscape when combined with dark borders.

INTERLOCKING STONE

Interlocking or pre-cast stone is a man-made product that has benefited greatly from recent innovation. In the early '70's, a sea of salmon-colored, brick-shaped pavers was commonplace in residential landscapes as an alternative to asphalt. Rather than conferring character on the landscape, they often drained it away. By contrast, today's interlocking stone offerings are as diverse as carpet choices and include dozens of different patterns, sizes, colors and textures.

In fact, the concept of "paver quilting," developed by Unilock, a Candian manufacturer, has gained wide acceptance by landscape professionals as well as homeowners. In paver quilting, you are offered a variety of choices for pattern, size, color and texture; you can then pick and choose and quilt them together. Anyone can mix and match colors or assemble patterns and mosaics to create high style, low maintenance pavers all their own. You're only limited by your imagination. Ease of installation is a hallmark of pre-cast stone, and people can get as creative as they like with these products; there are no rules for how they go together.

PROS:
1. Because it's pre-cast, there is a high level of quality control. Very few bricks in a batch are bad.
2. It's highly customizable.
3. There's a large palate of choices.
4. It's very easy to install, with low labor costs.
5. With respect to installation, there are no climate issues; you can install them in the rain.
6. Easily maintained: If something cracks or stains, they can be replaced with new ones.

CONS:
1. The larger sizes are difficult to manage and install.
2. Highly textured variations can be hard on wheelchairs or snow shovels.
3. Some tumbled stones create gaps large enough to snare a thin high heel.

5. Today, paver quilting is the popular choice in landscaping, both for industry professionals and landscape novices. **6.** Complex mosaics can be prepared using design aids provided by the manufacturer.

7. The installation of quilting designs can be very rewarding for the do-it-yourselfer. The detail and texture in the materials add an additional layer of complexity to the design. **8.** Paver quilting can be an effective way to add character to large settings.

GRAVEL

Gravel can be used effectively as a paving surface for walkways, driveways and patios. Traditionally, this isn't a popular choice for driveways, largely because it's difficult to maintain and especially to plow. Patios also present challenges for gravel, as any furniture can sink right into it. I tend to recommend gravel solely for walkways, although I have installed it elsewhere at the owner's request. Because it's not a finished product, it creates an informal, country affect. Any gravel surfacing or hardscaping will require a solid aggregate base to support it. (This entails layering crushed or clear gravel, which is used as a base for all hardscaping, beneath pea gravel, the more decorative pebbles with rounded edges.) You can get virtually any color, shape or size gravel for surfacing, from red-brick chips to white quartz stone.

Pea gravel is particularly effective. The purpose of this is to slow people down. Walking on pea gravel is like walking on marbles; your feet sink a bit. You'd want to use this on a walk through a rose garden, for example, where you want people to tarry. Dog runs are another good venue. There are hundreds of different types of gravel. At a building supply store, you'll be able to look through different choices.

If you want to use pea gravel within your garden, put filter cloth (felt) underneath it. This prevents the earth and weeds from coming up into the pea gravel and making a muddy or unsightly walkway.

1.

2.

3.

1. This colored gravel and matching flagstone border, or soldier course, is a great combination. The straight lines of the flagstone border add a formal component to this garden space. 2. Gravel laid without borders, as seen here, has a more informal feel; it's best for tertiary paths.

3. Because it is a difficult material to traverse quickly, gravel slows people down. In your journey through the garden, you can better appreciate other garden elements, such as water features or sculpture.

PROS:
1. It limits mobility, which is ideal for garden walkways.
2. Gravel is available in numerous colors, shapes and sizes.
3. It's one of the easiest hardscaping materials to install.
4. Visually, it works quite well for quiet areas of refuge.
5. It drains very well.

CONS:
1. Not wheelchair accessible.
2. If you don't retain it on all four sides, it will keep pushing over its borders.
3. Every time somebody walks over it, it gets indented, requiring regular maintenance.
4. Every year you should purchase new gravel and top it off.
5. It's loose. Car wheels can kick out stones, and kids can throw them.

4.

5.

6.

4. You will rarely find standing water or puddles on gravel walkways. It is a naturally porous material, and since added wieght does not compact it, it allows water to flow through to the ground below. **5.** Gravel is often used for dry stream beds. With the addition of larger stones, this feature looks at home next to a pond.

6. When gravel is used as a jointing material between stepping-stones, it will define the edges of the flagstone. Gravel accentuates the stone, much like grass but with less maintenance.

You can easily achieve a well-integrated garden enclosure by adding decorative columns, an overhead structure and by painting it all to match the color of the house.

CHAPTER 3

ENCLOSURE
PERGOLAS, ARBORS, GAZEBOS, WALLS & FENCES

The magic of garden planning is this: All you need to do is add a wall, a fence, a pergola, and suddenly you have an intimate space where none previously existed. These elements frame your outdoor experience—and

often with just the slightest suggestion of enclosure. Separated from the house, perhaps just by the stepping-stones of a path, an arbor can be an entrance that is really more an invitation to explore than a means of egress. A stone wall along the periphery of your property, on the other hand, may double as both a decorative feature and a method for keeping the deer from your garden.

Enclosure in the outdoors can be very functional, as anybody with a pool and small children can attest. But because the outdoors is best viewed as an opportunity to enjoy the unenclosed, I tend to view these elements also as subtle tools for shaping our outdoor experiences. If porches, terraces and decks represent the core of our hardscape, enclosure—in tandem with softscape and walkways—creates the full flow of space, both visually and physically. Whether it is a garden gate directing traffic or a gazebo offering a moment to take in a view, enclosure should dictate how we move and what we see.

PERGOLAS AND ARBORS

When landscape designers talk about garden rooms, they cite the need to think about flooring (lawns and terraces), walls (fences, hedges and walls) and, of course, ceilings (trees and awnings). Arbors and pergolas provide two of these features, walls and ceilings, in the most delightful manner.

Both pergolas and arbors are open, airy architetural-structures, sometimes constructed of wood or bamboo, sometimes of metal. Both are intended to be covered with wisteria, jasmine, clematis or some other fabulous climbing vine or flower. They can cover paths or terraces, or frame a particularly attractive view. In a garden, they can be a sort of living architecture. Unless they have been solidly roofed with a material such as Plexiglas, they are generally not weatherproof. Yet, on a sunny day they offer both shade and shelter.

Pergolas act as great transitions from one garden room to another and become one with the landscape as they are weathered by the years.

Arbors can draw you down a garden path. In this garden space, a focal
point at one end further draws the attention of the garden visitor.

An arbor can also act as a gateway, inviting us into another section of the garden.

Though the terms arbor and pergola are often used interchangeably, the accepted difference is that arbors cover passageways and pergolas define spaces. Arbors can be extended archways or long tunnels; pergolas can begin at the side of the house and extend as far as you'd like. Indeed, the word pergola comes from Latin *pergula*, meaning "projection." Arbors hark from Italy, where they were designed to hold ripening grapes and provide shade. They eventually made their way into English gardens, where they have been a fixture ever since.

Arbors and pergolas can be made from columns of wood, brick, stone stucco or cement. Their "roofs," generally open structures designed to support plants, can be of wood or metal. In his garden in Atlanta, landscape designer Ryan Gainey created an arbor with nothing more than bark covered by twigs and branches. Los Angeles-based landscape architect Michael Schneider of Orange Street Studios created a metal pergola that literally grows out of a terrace railing. The same posts that support the railing continue up to support a leafy ceiling of vines. This technique "creates windows," says Schneider.

The scale of arbors and pergolas should be determined by the setting—the house they are near, the other garden structures and the vistas they frame. If a table and chairs are going to be placed beneath an arbor or pergola, you'll need adequate room for circulation. The larger the garden structure, the more plantings will be required to clothe it. In general, however, pergolas and arbors are better when they're larger. They're such appealing places to sit that you don't want to make them too skimpy.

Above: Transition need not be boring. A pergola can be a very decorative element within the landscape, creating a distinct experience as one passes beneath it. **Opposite:** A gazebo, properly placed within the landscape, can act as a retreat or private refuge, as well as a decorative element in the natural setting.

Pergolas can also mask architectural issues. When a client was unhappy with the view from a second-floor dining room, which looked out over an asphalt roof, landscape architects Jennifer Booher and Bobbie Burdick created a weatherproof pergola. Since the house was a very formal colonial revival, they designed a structure with white columns and roofed it with a metal frame that held acrylic panels from Cyro, a company that specializes in sunroom glazing.

GAZEBOS

What sets a gazebo apart from pergolas and arbors is that it has a definite roof. An inherently more formal structure, a gazebo is a modern form of the Japanese teahouse and the Chinese garden room.

Some say the word gazebo comes from the Latin videbo, or "I shall see." Designer Peter Joel Harrison offers another opinion in his pattern book *Gazebos and Trellises: Authentic Details for Design and Restoration.* In 18th-century England, he explains, the aristocracy was besotted with French style. Thus, when a hostess heard a guest remark upon the beauty of her tea house by saying, "Ça, c'est beau," she whispered to a friend that the new French term for tea house must be "gazebo." Apparently the mangled phrase caught on.

A gazebo can be rustic, perhaps with a farmhouse tin roof, or it can be columned and formally shingled. It can be outfitted with a dinner party's supply of tables and chairs or casually lined with built-in benches. Some gazebos float on rafts in lakes. Others have ceiling fans whirring lazily to stir the breeze. Still others have wet bars, grills, sound systems and many of the amenities of home.

The secret to a successful gazebo? It needs to be on a path where people want to go. While other elements of enclosure serve more as signposts in your garden's flow, the gazebo is truly a destination. The route to and from it will determine whether it is useful or simply ornamental.

DESIGN TIP

Before you think about a high wall or a fence, check your local building codes. Most municipalities have rules for building on property lines. If you're planning a freestanding wall, you may violate codes if you don't dig a foundation or reinforce it with steel. A quick call to the building department or a look at your town's website can eliminate many unforeseen problems.

WALLS

Walls in a landscape can be a structural necessity or a means of creating visual intrigue. They can solve a site problem, create a demarcation between spaces, or visually balance out a landscape. Whether they are made of stone, brick, stucco or other materials, they are usually the boldest feature in the landscape and an important element of the overall design. Whatever their purpose, they have to be properly constructed and able to withstand seasonal changes.

There are two primary types of walls. Retaining walls are used on hilly properties to buttress earth and carve out flat space for living and gardening. Determining the height of the retaining wall and the number of terraced areas you'll need depends on the steepness of your slope. If you're trying to level a gentle incline, one retaining wall generally will be sufficient. If you're faced with a steep slope, you'll need to create a series of terraced lawns or gardening areas accompanied by steps.

Freestanding walls have many uses. They can shield the barbecue pit from the wind, support a climbing vine, mark the property lines, keep out the neighbor's dogs, block the view of a nearby highway or separate the dining area from the volleyball court. Most important, their purpose is to partition spaces. In this role, walls, like fences, don't necessarily have to be high or elaborate. I've seen effective constructions that were barely curbhigh. Even a row of boulders or a stack of firewood can act as a wall in the landscape, creating a sense of enclosure without actually closing off the space. If money is an issue, masonry walls can be built low and topped with a higher wooden fence.

Opposite: Walls can be designed to work in harmony with fences. This wall breaks up a section of fence that could become monotonous, creating a private garden room. **Above:** When considering materials for a wall, first think of its purpose. If it is being used as a retaining wall, as shown here, heavier construction materials, such as stone, should be considered.

MATERIALS FOR WALLS

Brick, concrete, stone, stucco: Almost any material that can be piled up and made to stay that way can be used to create a wall. But don't let that over-simplification seduce you. The difference between the right material and the almost right material can be substantial. And always, the first requirement in designing a wall is that it serves as an architectural extension of your house, both in terms of style and material.

Brick

Brick is one of the more common materials used for walls, largely because of the variety of colors and sizes available and relatively low installation costs. Before you order bricks, do a little research into the countless options available in your area. You'll probably be able to find everything from regular wire-cut, mass-produced varieties to expensive hand-molded and hand-cast bricks. Standard bricks are 2"x4"x8"; queen-sized bricks are 4"x4"x8"-9"; oversized bricks are 5"x4"x9".

Brick lends itself to wonderful patternings. A wall can be built with a herringbone pattern. Bricks can be laid on a 45-degree angle. A row of bricks

Opposite: A freestanding brick wall with a coping atop makes an inviting doorway to another garden room. Since the other side is not completely visible, this type of gateway creates an air of intrigue.
Above: Large armor stone boulders can be used in retaining walls to create terraces and reclaim land that previously was sloped.

laid in the same manner, also known as a soldier course, can go around the edges of the wall to frame the interior pattern like a picture frame. Bricks can also be laid in an open-weave pattern so that the wind can blow through.

In determining what design you'd like for a brick wall, first keep in mind the architectural style of your house. Second, consider whether you want the wall to be prominent in the landscape. If you plan on having plants hide it, it can be simple. If you want it to be a feature, you'll probably want to construct it with a high level of detail, perhaps even with a built-in fountain or sculpture.

One thing to keep in mind when building with bricks: Since bricks are geometric, a wall will need to be stepped if it is to follow the curves in a landscape. Brick walls are also weather-susceptible at both their base and their mortar joints. A good footing and a proper foundation are necessary to prevent any movement in sub-freezing temperatures.

Materials can dictate the look of a wall and help to set the theme within the garden. Here, reclaimed stone artifacts that have been worked into the wall help achieve the desired effect of a ruin.

Concrete

Since concrete can be molded to take any form, it is more adaptable than stone and brick. It can be easily curved to follow a sinuous line in a garden, or it can be designed so that it has regular windows or elaborate openwork.

Concrete can also be colored and textured in a variety of ways and can be shaped variously, using Fiberglas or wood molds. Still, despite concrete's obvious strength and versatility, we don't see much in the way of concrete garden walls, with the exception of poolside applications, largely because of the expense involved in construction. (For more detailed information on concrete options, see *Materials Quick Tour 1*.)

Stucco

One popular finish for concrete walls is stucco. A staple of architectural styles ranging from Mediterranean and Prairie to Tudor and colonial, stucco walls are crafted around a core of cement block or wood framework. They can be left smooth on top or finished with wood or flat stones. As a finishing touch, the stucco, which is usually white, can be tinted a soft pastel. Or it can be painted when it dries. Stucco can also be used in combination with other materials. Last year, we designed a wall along a property line that had brick columns, big barn beams and recessed stucco panels.

Stone

Historically, stone has been the material used most often to build walls in the landscape, and that continues to be the case today. Stone weathers very well and has a timeless quality and universal appeal. Stone varies widely in its properties, colors, cuts and, for wall applications, in the way it's stacked. Wall stone is available in five forms: limestone, sandstone, slate, granite and marble. Granite and marble are wonderful, if very costly, options. Most

homeowners choose sandstone, limestone or slate, basing their decision on their design and color goals. Slate comes in many hues, from purple and blue to black and gray. Limestone ranges from taupe and gray to orange. Sandstone is generally buff or tan.

Each of these types of stones can come in one of the following forms. They all have very different looks, so make sure you consider how each form would work in your wall before making your purchase. I always recommend evaluating the stone in your landscape to see how it blends in.

Building stone: Fieldstones of various sizes and shapes.

Rubble stone: Irregular stones with one good face that can be turned to the outside.

Dimensional stone: Stone cut to size in the yard, split-faced if required, and polished or finished to specification; used inside or outside. Also called cut stone or ashlar.

Monumental stone: Stones traditionally used for grave markers that can be either rough or finished. In walls, they are most often used as coping or capstones.

Flagstone: Flat slabs ranging in thickness from a half-inch to fourteen inches. Slabs can be sized and shaped to fit the application.

The form you use is a matter of personal preference because any structural differences are mitigated by proer methods of installation.

Concrete planter walls and seating walls are versatile to work with because they are poured into pre-constructed forms in their exact location. Although they are costly to install, they create contemporary architectural surfaces in garden settings.

Top: Natural stone used as a retaining wall can double as stairs.
Bottom left: Limestone boulders can be the perfect retaining wall material for large grade changes, as they maintain a natural appearance.
Bottom right: Where machine access and cost are an issue, natural stone can be used in an innovative manner to hold back a grade change.

Pre-Cast Wall Stone

Pre-cast stone is cement mixed with a fine aggregate, such as sand, that is then colored and formed into various shapes. At one time, pre-cast retaining wall units were designed as a one-sided product that could be used only for retaining slopes. Now the manufacture of pre-cast stone has been refined, and it is available as a freestanding wall material that can be approached from two sides.

The advantage to using pre-cast stone in either freestanding or retaining walls is that it is lighter in weight and eliminates the need to set a wall on a foundation or concrete footing. It can be installed simply on a bed of compacted gravel. (For more on pre-cast stone, see Chapter 4, *Access*, to learn how it is used in walkways.)

Mortar Matters

The color mortar you choose has a dramatic effect on the look of a wall. To draw attention to the mortar and make the patterning of the wall prominent, choose a color that is much lighter or darker than your brick or stone. To make the mortar disappear visually, choose a color that is a very close match to the brick or stone. When in doubt, go neutral. Gray or charcoal works with most stone. Terra cotta, a blend of three colors, is great with brick. Taupe works well with limestone or sandstone.

The thickness of your mortar will affect the look of your wall, too. The thicker the joint, the more it will stand out. Similarly, mortar that oozes around the edges of the brick or stone will be more prominent. Even though oozing mortar gives plants something to grab onto, I'm not a big fan of this material. In most cases, I prefer a recessed joint, one in which the mortar has been pushed back 3/8" or 1/2" by a joining tool. Another standard finish is a trowel finish, where the mortar is flush with the brick or stone.

From top to bottom: (1) Walls need not be one-sided. In fact, when a wall extends up from its retaining feature, it can act as a seating wall where it meets the terrace. (2) Freestanding natural stone walls mortared into place create a formal entry environment to most any home. The neutral gray tones blend in with most house façades. (3) Combining pre-cast walls and stairs with natural stone landings can create a beautiful, yet cost-effective seating area. (4) Pre-cast wallstone can be engineered to fit most grade changes found in residential settings. (5) Once plants are set behind retaining walls, their colors and textures create a whole new dimension.

- Instead of a railing on top of a high wall, plant shrubs to keep guests from wandering to the wall's edge.
- Follow the lead of Gertrude Jekyll, the great English gardener, and add pockets of soil to dry or wet laid walls so they'll cascade with flowers. Mulleins, foxgloves and columbines work well for wall gardening, especially if grown from seeds sprinkled between the rocks.
- Cover a wall with vines by inserting a series of hooks or nails into the mortar of a brick or stone wall. They should be placed vertically, one foot above the other. Wires can be run between the hooks or nails to encourage vines to travel upward.
- Build a custom planter, either by adding one to the face of the wall or designing a planter pocket in the top of that wall, so you can nurture cascading vines and flowers. Frank Lloyd Wright typically incorporated planters in his walls.
- Treat a wall as a plant gallery, and install pots or planters on brackets.

The Art of the Stone Wall

There are two types of stone walls: dry and wet laid. The former dates from colonial times, when farmers harvested rocks from their flinty fields and piled them one upon another to build walls that are still admired by landscape designers. Today, creating a dry laid stonewall is considered a true art form.

To build a dry stonewall, stones are placed tightly together; in the best walls no space is larger than two inches. They are chinked with nothing more than a little soil and slivers of stone. The weight of the stones creates a wall so strong that it can buttress earth. Thus, in addition to marking boundaries of terraces, fields and garden rooms, dry stone walls are often used as retaining walls. They are an asset in cold climates because they can shift up and down freely as the ground freezes and thaws.

If you talk to a stone wall connoisseur like David Reed, a North Carolina artisan and author of *The Art and Craft of Stonescaping*, you'll discover that not every stone wall is a good one. The best have a top that is even and level. They are wider at the bottom than the top. They are set into the ground at least four to six inches so that they "appear to grow out of the ground, not balance on it." If a wall is meant for retaining earth, it should tilt back into the ground it supports at a rate of 1/8" per foot of height. If it is freestanding, it should be similarly tapered on both sides. Good proportions for a freestanding wall are two feet wide and three feet high or three feet wide and four feet high. Wet or dry stone walls can be laid with fieldstone or quarried rock. Local rock is generally the best to choose.

According to Reed, wet laid stone walls, which entail adding mortar to the stone, are a sin. Mortar inevitably cracks as the ground shifts. Not only that, it binds itself more or less permanently to rocks, assuring they will never be adequately recycled in a future generation.

But craftsmen with the skills to lay a dry wall are not as plentiful as masons. Often, mortar-bound walls are a homeowner's only option. Fortunately, wet laid stone walls generally cost less, partly because they require less stone.

Booher and Burdick use wet laid stone walls as a "veneer" on concrete walls. They are careful to craft their wet laid walls so that the mortar is recessed two to three inches behind the stone. "When shadows hit, it looks like they're dry laid," says Booher. This technique is called "raking the joint."

Fieldstone can be a very cost-effective wall to build, since most rural environments have access to this type of stone at a low cost per ton. By placing plant material in cracks, the gruff appearance of the stone can also be softened.

Microclimates: Because walls, fences and hedges provide shelter from the wind, they create microclimates around them. But walls offer more than just shelter. They absorb heat during the day and radiate it at sunset. Snowdrops planted next to a south-facing stone wall will bloom earlier than those in an exposed part of the garden. Similarly, summer blooms will last a little longer in a walled garden.

Above: White picket-style fencing can draw visitors' attention, and with the inclusion of plant material here, a certain level of surprise is introduced. **Opposite:** If the focus is on something other than the wooden fence, go with weathered or stained rails because they blend more into the landscape.

FENCES

Fences, traditionally made of wood, are usually simpler, less expensive and faster to construct than stone, brick, stucco or concrete walls. They can be easily customized to partition space, hide a view or camouflage any number of unsightly things, ranging from air-conditioning units and compost bins to trash sheds and service areas. In urban settings, fences are essential for privacy and security. In country or suburban settings, they provide a safe zone for children and dogs, and help keep vegetables away from groundhogs and deer. But aside from fences' utilitarian purposes, gardeners like them because they add architectural interest to a natural setting. With interesting decorative caps called finials—vintage ones are widely available at flea markets—or metal grillwork, fences can be landscaping works of art in their own right.

Fence heights generally range from three-and-a-half feet to six feet. Three or four feet is a good height if you're fencing in children and pets. For privacy, six feet will be necessary. Security fencing needs to be eight feet high.

The design of a fence should be determined by its use. Where views are attractive, you'll want a fence with lots of openness—perhaps split rails, pickets or a Chinese Chippendale pattern. When views are unattractive, you'll need a high, solid fence, such as a stockade fence or a tight board fence with a lattice top. These can be softened with plantings, vines, espaliered trees, tall shrubs or a grove of leafy bamboo. In considering what style of fence to choose, ask yourself whether you plan to make the fence a feature or whether it is simply a necessary partition that should be a backdrop to your plantings.

Unless camouflaged by plants, fences tend to dominate a landscape. Thus, if you're fencing a large area, you'll want to break up a fence's unremitting horizontal line with a gate, even if it is a gate to nowhere. You can reduce the impact of a high fence by adding windows, perhaps to highlight a view of a field garden beyond.

As with garden furniture, a fence that is painted white will call far more attention to itself than one made of weathered wood. That's why designer Bunny Williams likes to stain fences a medium gray. If she's trying to hide them with plants, she'll add a layer of lattice in front, stained a slightly lighter gray, and then train vines up it. The basic rule of thumb on fence color: Dark hues will make a fence recede; light and bright colors will make it stand out.

Fence Styles

Here are some basic fence styles:

Close-board fence: Classically, the close-board fence is a handsome wall of boards set off by posts topped with finials. Today, however, privacy is most often accomplished by a high stockade fence, which can be a mundane backdrop for a garden. Williams transforms such fences by using large square posts topped with a finial between the panels, making enclosures that look "quite civilized."

Post-and-rail fence: This common garden fence is a post with holes cut out to hold three rails. Post-and-rail fences can also be made with diagonal or chinoiserie patterns. For a rustic look, bark can be left on the rails.

Split-rail fences: Because the horizontal supports are rough-hewn, split-rail fences evoke the great frontier. Regional patterns vary. In Virginia, split-rail fences zigzag; in Wyoming, they crisscross.

Woven fences: Interwoven strips of wood, willow branches or wicker can create the effect of a garden set in a large basket. Woven willow fences are called wattle and create a casual look that is sought after in country and kitchen gardens. They are not extremely durable and need to be replaced after several years.

Bamboo screen: A sleek contemporary option, the bamboo screen weathers to a soft gray.

DESIGN TIP

If you want to block the wind, don't erect a high, solid fence. The wind will merely whip over the fence and attack your plants with undiminished force. A better option is a hedge that filters the wind, or a slatted fence or honeycomb brick wall. These will slow the force of the wind. Alternately, a forty-five-degree baffle or an angled section along the top of the fence will mitigate the wind.

Lattice: A crisscross of wood laths, lattice can come in diagonal or geometric patterns. Because of its airiness, it can be used on its own as a sort of screen. Or it can be set in front of a wood fence or masonry wall and used for training flowers, vines or vegetables. The best lattice is notched, not overlapped, so that it creates one smooth wall.

Picket fences: Though we now associate picket fences with colonial America (not to mention Tom Sawyer), these see-through fences were features in Chinese pleasure grounds two centuries ago. The pickets can be simple boards, or they can have rounded and decorative tops. They can be uniform in height or create a graceful curve from post to post. The fence posts, likewise, can be plainly capped, left unadorned or embellished with cutouts.

Iron fences: Ornate cast- and wrought-iron screens and railings were originally the preserve of cathedrals. During the Industrial Revolution, the fanciful possibility of the material intrigued the Victorians. Iron fence styles range from Gothic to Chippendale to rustic. Many contemporary artists work in the medium, making custom motifs to suit particular gardens.

Chain link: Cheap but undeniably practical, chain link doesn't rate high on the aesthetic totem pole. But painted green so that it blends in with the garden, it can be disguised by a planting—perhaps vines or a bamboo grove. Another way to disguise chain link is to put a slightly higher fence in front of it. It is a good support for lattice or wattle.

Flea Market Finds

You would be surprised at what you can find at an old junkyard or a flea market. In fact, I often meet my welder at the scrap yard to scavenge for reinforcement bars of steel, bent metal, sheets of aluminum or pieces of copper and bronze that have been removed from buildings or salvaged from machinery. At a metal scrap yard, these items are purchased in bulk by weight. You will find that you will get useful materials at a fraction of their true cost. These items can then be used within a landscape to create works of art or points of interest. You can construct pergolas or arbors. You can weld metal and found objects into walls that are part sculpture. This is a particularly good way to create interest in an urban garden. I've even found that a leftover sheet of galvanized roofing can make an interesting wall. When I find steel items, I like to allow them to rust so as to create another layer of color and interest.

On one recent trip, I came across some highly decorative antique heater grates, intended for the inside of a house. I bought all those available, even though I still had no idea what to do with them. Eventually they were used as peek-holes in a wooden privacy gate, and had we not had them on hand, that fence would never have been born.

Alternatives to Walls and Fences

If you want to partition space but you don't want anything as substantial as a wall or a fence, try:

- Putting a railing on a terrace or garden path
- Planting a bramble of blackberries or wild roses to act as a barrier
- Changing the elevation of your garden by adding a sunken terrace or a raised deck
- Adding an edging, perhaps a curb of cement, cobblestone or railroad ties
- Altering the size of your paths and their paving material, i.e., swapping flagstone for brick or vice versa
- Planting a grove of trees, shrubs or leafy bamboo
- Building a "ha-ha," a formal garden term for a trench that separates a garden and a field beyond; think of a ha-ha as a nouveau moat, a boundary that cows— and people—can see over but won't cross
- Creating a visual boundary, a focal point that stops the eye—and traffic.

Opposite: Fences can be built around an arbor to create a more formal entry or gateway into a different garden room

GATES

Everyone is instinctively drawn toward a gate. Like an arch, a gate frames a view and creates the idea that there is someplace to go, even if it only opens onto a small suburban yard. A white gate in a green hedge will instantly be a focal point. A gate topped with a vine-covered archway will lend presence to a pool or backyard entrance.

In designing a gate, it is important to take into account the architectural style of your house. A fanciful wrought-iron gate will look out of place on a ranch house. A rustic twig gate will look more appropriate leading to a vegetable garden than to a formal terrace.

Gates should be wide enough that people and wheelbarrows can pass through. They should be made of pressure-treated or rot-proof lumber. The hinges and fasteners should be rust- or stain-proof.

Previous page: Fencing can be designed to formalize a garden space. Here, the fence, gate and arbor are a single, integrated unit that connects the main house to additional living space. **Above:** On the other hand, with natural materials or finishes, fences and gates can blend seamlessly into the garden.

4 BASICS

1.

Enclosure adds a new dimension to the landscape. Before adding an enclosure, most yards are what architects call a ground plane—a platform, in other words. After an enclosure is erected, a landscape takes on a three-dimensional aspect that makes it much more visually interesting—and often more functional.

2.

Even the most rustic enclosure is a feat of engineering. So, as carpenters like to say, measure twice, cut once. Be exact, and consult with a structural engineer if you're in doubt about whether the enclosure will withstand the tests of time and the elements.

3.

Enclosures can open space up, not just close it off. The space behind the enclosure used to be next to the space in front of the enclosure. Now it's beyond it. Enclosures offer visual perceptions of different spaces within a single landscape.

4.

Use enclosures with restraint. If you use too many enclosures, or enclosures that are too long or too high, the yard will seem like a maze rather than a comfortable, usable space.

NATURAL STONE

Because of its inherent beauty and natural longevity, stone has long been a favorite of landscape architects and designers. Stone weathers very well, and it has a timeless quality and universal appeal. From rustic hedgerows to elaborate masonry, stone is found on walls throughout the world. Stone varies widely in its properties, colors, cuts and, for wall applications, in the way it's stacked. Stone is broken down into forms and types (see below). The form you use is a matter of personal preference. The type of stone, however, will have definite implications for how well your hardscaping weathers and ages. Granite, for example, will go many years without requiring maintenance, even when highly polished. Limestone is subject to heave and scarring but is soft enough to accept gouges gracefully. Slate resists chemicals but fractures easily, while sandstone is much like limestone, and marble is even harder than granite. So be aware of the subtle differences in types as you select natural stone for your design.

Natural stone is available as rock, rough-cut or precise quarry-cut pieces. Most natural stone can be purchased in random rectangular patterns, meaning that all of the pieces are cut with right angles in various standard sizes—typically (in 6" increments) 6" x 6", 12" x 12", 12" x 18", 24" x 24", 24" x 30", etc. Random patterns look natural and neat at the same time and can be particularly appealing. For a more rustic effect, use a variety of sizes and chip them on site into uneven shapes that fit into the contours of adjacent pieces. This creates a jigsaw puzzle effect, and while the process is a little more labor-intensive, it results in a much more informal look.

1.

2.

3.

1. Natural flagstone is a classic stone option. A great benefit to using this sedimentary stone is its longevity with proper maintenance. 2. It takes a master mason to construct walls without the use of mortar. Europe has established a strong masonry tradition, with many structures standing for centuries.

3. Randomly laid flagstone is commonly used for walkways and patios. This type of installation generally establishes an informal setting.

4.

5.

6.

Forms of Stone

Virtually every kind of stone is available in one of the following seven forms:

- Building stone: Fieldstones of various sizes and shapes.
- Rubble stone: Irregular stones with one good face that can be turned to the outside.
- Dimension stone: Stone cut to size in the yard, split-faced if required, and polished or finished to specifications. Also called cut stone or ashlar.
- Monumental stone: Stones traditionally used for grave markers that can be either rough or finished.
- Flagstone: Flat slabs ranging in thickness from 1/2" to as much as 1 foot. Slabs can be sized and shaped to fit the application.
- Crushed stone: Normally, this is the gravel used as a compacted base for all hardscaping.

Thickness of Flagstones

Flagstone is by far the most popular form of stone. If you're using it, thickness is one of the main issues. Here are some basic guidelines:

- 1/2"to 2" thick: Used to mortar onto concrete.
- 2" to 3" thick: Used for walkways without a concrete base.
- 4" to 6" thick: Used for driveways without a concrete base.
- 6" to 8" thick: Used for steps.
- Random combination from 2" to 12": Used to form walls.
- Flagstone can also be purchased *guillotined* (straight cut), *rock-faced* (edges are hand-chipped with a hammer and chisel) or *quarried* (just as they come out of the ground), for varying degrees of formality.

4. The random flagstones on this patio have saw-cut edges. This establishes a semiformal setting but can be a labor-intensive installation. **5.** Select stones that are indigenous to your area; they blend in better with the natural surroundings. Curves can be created through a chipping process.

6. Flagstone stepping-stones can be ordered or purchased from a quarry in virtually any size or thickness.

Types of Stone

The stone materials that hardscapers prefer to use can vary in important ways. Here are the basics:

GRANITE

Granite is a very hard, long-lived igneous stone. It comes in a variety of colors and is quarried only in certain parts of the world, which means it may have to be imported. Granite is largely unaffected by freeze/thaw cycles because of its density. Within the landscape, it's often set as cobblestones for walkways and patios, where it weathers beautifully without losing its durability.

1.

PROS:
1. It is a beautiful material.
2. It's very long lasting, with virtually no maintenance.
3. Because it is such a dense stone, moisture can't penetrate it, making it impervious to freeze/thaw cycles.
4. Its surface can be manipulated, allowing for everything from a rough to a highly polished finish.
5. It has numerous uses in the landscape, from paving to outdoor kitchen countertops.
6. It is impervious to stains; you only need a brush and water to remove any stain.

2.

CONS:
1. It is one of the most expensive hardscaping materials.
2. It has limited availability: There's normally a waiting period for product.
3. Because it's so heavy, it's difficult to install.

3.

1. Granite setts, or cobblestone as they are more commonly known, have been used throughout Europe for centuries. Its durability and variation in color is rapidly making it a favorite material in today's landscape. 2. Granite in its original state looks much like any other mass of dark igneous stone. In certain cases, dynamite must be used to allow room for access to build a home. Because of its density, it can be more cost effective to work around it, as these homeowners did. 3. Granite can be purchased in various colors and forms. Here, it is used as a retaining wall.

4.

5.

6.

MARBLE

Marble, at the other end of the spectrum, is a very hard, impermeable material that wards off all but the worst effects of moisture. Its many colors and beautiful veining are so varied that designers can find a near-perfect match for any residential environment. Marble is notoriously expensive to produce, however, and can deteriorate over time from the effects of erosion and pollution (marble is chemically sensitive). These factors more or less restrict its use to very high-end hardscapes and even then, to relatively sheltered areas, such as porches, verandas and patios. Marble is much more frequently found in interiors than exteriors. Its pros and cons are virtually the same as granite, except that marble will break down and wear over time. Visually, it offers veining and color variations that granite does not have.

LIMESTONE

Limestone is a sedimentary rock, about half as hard as granite. Not all limestone is created equal: Indiana limestone possesses the highest degree of machinability, which allows it to be shaped and textured at a very low cost. (In fact, so much of the limestone used in the U.S. is quarried in Indiana that it is sometimes referred to as the nation's building stone.) Because the stone is soft, however, it scars easily. For this reason architects prefer to use it for small, rich-looking projects like entrances or balconies, and you won't find many varieties on large surfaces such as patios or walls. For some people, limestone has regional associations with the American Southwest or Tuscany, and its earthy colors seem evocative of landscapes saturated with sun.

PROS:

1. Because of its popularity, it's universally available.
2. Since it's a relatively soft stone, you can chisel or hand tool it easily.
3. It has a very rich, grand look.

4. Limestone can be found in many forms, the most popular of which is random rectangles. This is often the perfect hardscaping material for walkways and patios of all sizes. 5. Thicker versions of limestone can be hand chiseled to create walls and stairs. Here, the chiseling can be seen in the actual stair risers where a rock face has been added to the character of the stone.
6. Limestone can also be found in a weathered state as well. Here, moss and plant material grow out of the stone itself. Normally, this version of limestone will be found in damp shady environments.

4. Because it's lighter, you can work on it on site.

5. It has a variety of uses in the landscape. Since it's widely used in home construction, limestone can help to integrate landscape design with a house's architecture.

CONS:

1. It is porous and thus vulnerable to freeze/thaw wherever there is moisture.

2. Lower grade limestone is prone to pop out, crack or shatter after a freeze.

3. It scars easily.

4. Color variety is limited.

5. Because it's porous, it will stain.

SANDSTONE

Another sedimentary rock that comes from the bottom of oceans and lakes, sandstone seems to be popular everywhere. Its natural coloration is neutral, ranging from gray to tan to buff to white. It is native to most geographies and relatively affordable. About as hard as limestone, it is very commonly used for paving residential landscapes because it's very durable, and its mellow tones blend nicely when used in combination with interlocking stone. In fact, most materials work well when used in proximity to sandstone. Because of its similarities to limestone, its pros and cons are virtually the same.

SLATE

Slate is produced in many surfaces, finishes and colors. Slate is resistant to most chemicals, which makes it desirable for ground surfaces, but it must be quarried much thinner than other types of stone, which limits its applications. One of the best and most traditional ways to use slate is as roofing tile.

PROS:

1. It can be found in a variety of colors.

2. It's fairly dense, so it will wear well in heavily trafficked areas.

1.

2.

3.

1. As a soft stone that can scar very easily, sandstone is perfect for a ruin setting. The natural elements will affect it much quicker than granite. Because of its softness, sandstone is easy to hand-tool. **2.** In its flagstone form, sandstone can be hand chiseled to give the edging a rock face feature. As it weathers, the stone may be chiseled yet again to give it a fresh, new look. **3.** As stepping stones, sandstone can be placed easily in the landscape. Use this stone in secondary walks since it will scar easily with constant traffic.

4.

5.

6.

3. It is resistant to stains and chemicals.

4. It has numerous uses in the landscape, as well as homebuilding.

5. Like granite, it can be used as a paving material or countertop material.

CONS:

1. It's normally quarried in thin layers, so it must be mortared onto concrete.

2. It will crack on top of a gravel base.

3. It's not as widely available as other types of stone.

4. It can normally only be laid horizontally.

5. Its compressive strength is only half that of granite.

Hardscaping Boulders

Below are the three main types of boulders used in landscaped settings. To make these boulders appear as though they belong in your backyard, walk out into nature and study natural rock outcroppings. In your own hardscape, you should try to mimic those outcroppings by staggering the boulders (rocks are not normally found in clean rows) and burying the bottom third of the rock.

• Armor stone: These are large, limestone boulders with sharp edges, shaped like cubes and with flat tops so they're easy to stack. (Larger ones are used to build seawalls.) In the landscape, they can be used for a variety of purposes, from accent pieces in planting beds to retaining walls. They come in a variety of sizes, from a half-ton up to ten tons.

• Weathered boulders: These are more rounded than armor stones and usually have moss growing on them. They're often found with holes and nooks that are ideal for planting perennials. These can be used in waterscapes and require a damp, shady environment to maintain the moss.

• Ledge rock: Long, flat pieces of white rock, traditionally used in waterfalls. They're inexpensive, but not commonly used in landscape design.

4. Armor stone boulders can range in weight and size. The most common boulders used for retaining walls usually weigh four to six tons. Used together with plantings, they can be very soft in appearance. **5.** Ledge rock is commonly used within water features. Thicker pieces can also be used to hold back small slopes, in the water or on land. **6.** Rounded boulders can be used in the landscape as accents. They can come from a stone quarry or be pulled out of a farmer's hedgerow. In this design by Burdick and Booher, the landscape architects found the boulders in a nearby blueberry field.

CHAPTER 4

ACCESS
WALKWAYS, STEPS & DRIVEWAYS

When you exit your front door or step out of your car, chances are your foot will connect with hardscape. Driveways, walkways and steps are essential to any landscape design because they direct how your outdoor

space is seen and used. Well planned, these avenues of circulation will enhance vistas and magnify the beauty of plantings. Poorly planned, they will leave your lawn with brown paths cut by mail carriers, children and those who insist on taking the short cut to the trash shed.

In this chapter, we'll discuss rules of thumb for the design of walkways, steps and driveways. We'll present concepts for creating mood and interest and principles for planning that will help you make sure these very permanent landscape features are as beautiful and practical as they can be.

WALKWAYS

Before you think about whether you want your path to be straight or curved, function must be considered. When I first began designing landscapes for shopping malls, I waited a year to install the paths because it's been my experience that people pick the strangest routes to travel by foot. At the end of the year, I would simply plan paths where the flowerbeds and lawn areas had been trampled.

In domestic settings, a year's wait is not necessary because the routes people will travel can be accurately anticipated. The average home will need one major walkway that leads from the driveway or sidewalk to the front door, and a secondary walkway that's primarily used to access the backyard. Additionally, some homes will need a tertiary walkway that's used less often—usually for

gardening, garbage storage or a dog run.

Primary and secondary walkways are usually made of a solid material, such as concrete, brick or interlocking stone, while tertiary walkways can be more adventurous and involve stepping-stones, pea gravel or even mown grass. The reason for the design differences stems from usage. Primary and secondary walkways get a lot of

Opposite: Varying materials for adjoining walkways will slow people down and make them more aware of the path that leads them in a different direction. **Right:** Natural pieces of limestone can be used to create not only stairs but also stepping-stones. Here, the inherent beauty of natural stone is enhanced by the transparency of the water.

traffic year-round. These are the paths everyone from toddlers to the elderly must negotiate, and the paths that must be shoveled and swept. They need to be solid and sturdy. A tertiary walkway is for strolling and admiring, and it can be more imaginative and less practical.

Walkways transform open space. They define centers of activity and increase the feeling of size in a garden. As the late English gardener Russell Page wrote: "Paths indicate the structure of a garden plan, and the stronger and simpler the lines they follow, the better."

Siting Walkways

Paths need to go somewhere and where they go is important. Before you plot your paths, it's important to position your garden elements: pools, terraces, arbors, utility sheds, large trees, perennial beds. Then consider your primary, secondary and tertiary walks as ways to link and define the character of these elements.

Primary paths should enhance the architecture of the house. They should echo the materials and style of the house. Visually, they should line up with front doors, backdoors and important windows, providing powerful

sight lines for viewing and exploring the garden. To draw the eye along a path, it is necessary to plan a focal point: a statue, a sundial, a fountain or a beautiful tree. (See Chapter 1, *Designing Outdoor Spaces*, for focal point ideas.)

Secondary pathways add mystery and surprise. Since they do not need to funnel guests to the house or driveway, they can meander. It is usually via a secondary pathway that a garden is viewed. By planning this path so that it passes by shrubs or flowering trees, you can ensure that the whole garden cannot be seen at once. The great English gardener Rosemary Verey noted, "Your garden must never reveal itself at a single glance; you should be able to walk round it experiencing constant feelings of surprise, anticipation and changing mood."

Tertiary walkways can head off to a utility shed, or they can cut through a perennial bed to give gardeners a place to crouch and weed. They can be narrow, perhaps a bluestone path. Often they are made of stepping-stones so that plantings grow up around them and the path becomes part of the garden.

Siting any walkway takes a thorough understanding of the terrain of your yard. It is important to walk the paths you are planning several times, by yourself and with other members of your family. Pay attention to gentle rises you may have previously neglected. Study the views and the effects of shadows and trees. Notice the places where water collects. Think about how a paving surface will look after rainfall—flagstone, for instance, acquires a shine after a light rain.

When you have a clear idea of where you'd like to mark out your paths, use a garden hose or rope to define the route. Then go inside and view the paths from any windows, even an attic window, to make sure they are in the right spot. And go outside in the garden to view the paths as they progress back to the house or the pool, or whatever their destination.

Previous page: In this contemporary home, the primary path as well as the driveway are made of concrete, helping them successfully integrate with the stucco house. **Above:** A tertiary pathway can be designed with less formal materials since it is usually located out of public view. Randomly laid flagstone with grass joints is a common solution.

10 TIPS FOR DESIGNING A FRONT WALK

1. The style of a front walk should be dictated by the house. The path should have a matching formality or informality, and it should echo the materials of the house. If the house is cottage style, random flagstones would be a good choice. If the house is formal, geometric stone or brick would be appropriate.

2. Front walks, with few exceptions, should follow the most direct route between the street and the door.

3. The path should be clearly visible and distinct from the grass and any curbside plantings. Neighbors strolling by should not have to search for a route to the door.

4. Front walks need to be wide. Two people with possessions need to be able to walk side by side. The minimum comfortable width for a front walk is four feet; I like to make mine five or even six feet wide, depending on the scale and proportions of the house and property.

5. The front landing, front steps or portico can help determine the maximum width of a walk. The path needs to be integrated into these architectural elements, but first consider the purpose of the walk. For example, will it simply be used to get from the driveway to the front door or is it to be used also as a seating area?

6. To enhance a visitor's arrival experience, pay attention to all the senses. Surround a front walk with fragrant plants. Rely on the trickle of a fountain to screen out street noises and signal that a soothing oasis of friendship is at hand.

7. Add an arbor or a gate to make the progress up a front path even more visually stimulating and to help create a separation between public and private spaces.

8. Trim any low tree branches that make navigating the path difficult.

9. Light the path with overhead lighting positioned on a tree or under a house eave. (See Chapter 6, *Decorating Outdoors*, for detailed lighting ideas.)

10. Make sure your front walkway has good drainage. No one appreciates puddles in warm weather or frozen patches of ice in cold. Plan paved paths so that they have a two percent slope away from the house.

The mood of a property is defined by the front walk and its associated landscape. Colors used in the exterior architecture of the home should be echoed in the soft and hard elements of the landscape.

Planted Walkways

The most obvious way to blend walkway and garden is to use stepping-stones and let low-growing herbs, such as creeping thyme or corsican mint, grow up around your stones. But walkways can blend with plantings in other ways.

Design your walkways with spaces between stones. Bricks and stones can be laid a few inches apart to allow grasses and herbs to grow up in the cracks. When the greenery is too high, the path can be mown as a lawn would be.

Bands of plantings can bisect paved walkways at regular intervals, a technique that will not only make the walk seem less formal but will also give it a different perspective, seeming to shorten it.

The ultimate planted walkway is a natural grass path or a path mown through a meadow or field. The latter solution works best in the summer because summer is the season for gardens and garden strolling.

Above: Planted joints between pieces of flagstone help to define stone edges and can be easily maintained by running a lawn mower across the top. **Opposite:** Large slabs of flagstone will help slow people down and make them more aware of the surroundings as they make their way through a garden.

Six Essentials of Walkway Design

1. **Match the style and scale of the walk to the architecture of your house.** If a house has brick or stone detailing, the walkways should reflect that. If you don't want to do a whole walkway in brick or stone, you can mix other materials—such as cement, gravel or pre-cast pavers—and use brick or stone as part of the patterning or as edging. (This technique is also known as laying a soldier course.) Remember, the larger the house, the larger the scale of the walkway.

2. **Match the material you choose to the mood you want.** If you want a straight path, it doesn't have to be formal. You can give it a different mood by using more casual materials, such as stepping-stones or bricks interplanted with grass.

3. **Pay attention to edging.** Just as a frame changes the look of a picture, so edging can alter the character of a path. A border of brick or stone can dress up gravel. A romantic sweep of perennials give formal paving a soft new look. When a path cuts through a lawn, a flat edging (preferably from stone, used as a soldier course) is essential so that a mower wheel can travel along the path and cut the shaggy grass that grows at the edges, thus eliminating the need for a weed whacker.

4. **Use color to make a path a focal point—or make it recede from view.** A path of white, light or colorful gravel will draw attention to itself, as will a path in a bright mosaic of small stones or tile. Similarly, a path of wood chips or earth-colored cement will recede from view.

5. **Use paving patterns to alter the character of your path.** Paving laid in long, straight lines will draw the eye onward. Paving set with a horizontal or diagonal pattern will make the path seem wider and keep the eye focused on the immediate. So too an intricate pattern creates intimacy.

6. **Change paving materials when you want to change the mood.** A change from gravel to brick, or tile

Above: Pre-cast stone can be customized with a variety of patterns, colors and shapes, as these walkways manufactured by Unilock illustrate.
Opposite: These stepping-stones, used in conjunction with large slab steps, blend naturally into the landscape. This path, rather than being imposed on the land, becomes part of it.

DESIGN TIP

To make the most of the vistas your pathways offer, replace solid front or back doors with glass-paned ones. Or enlarge a doorway so that you can install French doors and make a gracious transition out to the garden.

to colored aggregate is one of the best ways to make visitors feel they have entered a new and different part of the garden. One of my design professors tells the story of the time he was hired by a storekeeper who had recently taken over a business and was having trouble getting people to notice his store. He hoped that new landscaping would help. This client became somewhat alarmed when my professor failed to install any exotic plants, flowering trees or painted iron benches. In fact, all the architect did was remove the cement sidewalk and replace it with bluestone. As people walk or drive, he explained, they subconsciously monitor the ground ahead. A change in pavement quite literally gives them pause and causes them to look around for what's new. It worked; people began to notice the store, and business soared.

Path Materials

Some choices for path materials:

Stone: Though traditionally a formal solution, stone can take on a different character if, for instance, a medley of rocks is used as a border. It need not be laid with strict geometry. A crazy quilt of flagstone can be used for a path. The more intricate the pattern, the more it will slow visitors as they walk.

Pre-cast stone: Pre-cast stone, or interlocking stone as it is better known, has come a long way since its inception. There are dozens of different choices you can make when using this material. A pre-cast walkway can be made to look very informal (circle patterns), old world (cobblestone), creative and unique (paver quilting) or very formal (granite-like finishes), all at a very reasonable cost.

Stepping-stones: These can be made of rustic stones, smooth slices of tree trunks, millstones (with their centers possibly filled in with cement), pre-cast pavers, broken concrete or any material that can be dry laid. They can be used to link pathways, providing a loose and easy transition between diverse materials.

Brick: A traditional material for walks to vegetable and herb gardens, bricks can have a quaint or formal feel. Countless patterns are possible, including herringbone and basket-weave motifs. Bricks can be used wide-side-up or, as Gertrude Jekyll and Edwin Lutyens preferred, with the long narrow sides visible.

On a large property, a series of stone slabs can create "stepping-stone terraces." For example, while designing the grounds for a country estate, we found large slabs of stone at the back of the property, where land had recently been cleared. We set them into the grass along established travel patterns to serve as small terraces. This stepping-stone arrangement facilitated movement from one area to another and could easily be cleared of mud or snow. Installation required no excavation and almost no money.

Top: Concrete is probably the most widely used pathway material because of its longevity and low cost of installation. **Middle:** Gravel comes in virtually any size, shape and color. It gives a rural feeling when installed, though a hard edge is required to contain it. **Bottom:** Schneider added patterned pebbles to this concrete walkway.

They can readily be combined in decorative patterns with concrete slabs, cobbles or a wide range of other materials.

Gravel: For paths that don't need to be shoveled during winter snows or swept in leaf season, gravel is an attractive choice. To keep gravel in place, especially if the stones are small, an edging of wood, stone or metal may be necessary. The finer the gravel, the simpler maintenance will be. If the path will need to be raked, gravel should be no more than a half-inch in diameter.

Decomposed granite: Made of pulverized granite with grains that are similar to a larger version of sand, decomposed granite, or DG, is the material used on the walks along the Champs-Elysées. It can be ordered with a stabilizer so it sets like cement, though its top surface will still have particles that shake loose.

Patterned pebbles: Dress up a concrete path with patterns of pebbles. You can create monograms, leaves, nautilus-like spirals, whirling stripes, or formal geometric designs. The pebbles need to be placed by a professional. If they sink, the pattern disappears; if they protrude, walking is difficult.

Concrete: Since concrete is poured into forms, it can be used to make stepping-stones, slabs or curving paths. A skilled mason can work the "cream" of the concrete, making patterns with trowel marks or creating impressions with leaves or fronds. He also can add such finishing touches as aggregate, seashells or pebbles. Landscape architect Michael Schneider likes to add tumbled glass or mica chips to the surface of his concrete paths.

Broken concrete: This material, made of recycled fragments from concrete driveways, is good for stepping-stones. "It's fun to see score joints [e.g., the lines scored to keep large expanses of concrete from cracking] running in various directions," says Schneider, who likes to use broken concrete in varying colors.

Wood: For paths that extend over uneven or wet

terrain, a wooden boardwalk is an excellent solution. Be aware, though, that wood can be slippery when wet.

Organic materials: For tertiary paths, a variety of organic materials can be used. Depending on your location, you can choose from licorice root, shredded pine bark, cocoa beans, nut hulls, ground corncobs, wood chips and crushed seashells. The softer the material, the more sound it absorbs and the quieter a garden will seem. However, the softer the material, the more quickly it will need replenishing.

Packed earth: In dry climates, the well-trodden path can be left unadorned. Even in wet climates, the old cow path is a good solution for walks that are far from a house or off in woodland settings.

Square flagstone creates a sense of formality when laid in a modular fashion. When stepping-stones are set flush in a lawn, a lawnmower can easily run over the top.

Due to water's reflective nature, its presence in a landscape enlarges perceived space. Here, the simple addition of a wood bridge, designed to float over the pond, is an inspiration worthy of Monet.

Walkway Construction Basics

Walkways need to be set on a proper compacted granular base. To lay them on topsoil is a mistake, since the ground or topsoil will absorb moisture, expanding and contracting as the thermometer dips above and below freezing, thus shifting any material that is sitting on top of it. Therefore, it is essential to dig down at least six inches for a pedestrian walkway, until you get below the topsoil or organic layer of earth. Depending on the type of walkway you've decided to construct, you may need to dig even deeper.

Always consider drainage when installing walkways. Surface drainage may not be sufficient; you may also need an underground drainage layer, depending on the material used for the walkway. Make sure to consult a professional for advice before digging. Here are some quick tips on constructing a variety of walks:

Stone walks require a sturdy base that consists of six inches of compacted crusher run gravel. This is limestone screening, also known as stone dust, mixed with larger, 3/4" or 5/8" gravel. When combined, watered and compacted, this material produces a very solid base for walkways. On top of that is placed a setting bed of coarse sand. Usually an inch or so is placed on top of the gravel base and then screeded, or leveled, to create a flat surface on which to lay the proposed stone. Then the stone is manually (or, in the case of a large area, mechanically) placed on top of the sand bed in a pre-chosen pattern. Once the stone is placed and all cutting is complete, the entire area is sand swept with clean brick sand or a polymer sand that will keep weeds from germinating between the cracks of the stone. Finally, a plate tamper (compacter) is run over the top of the sanded, interlocking stone and all excess sand is swept away.

Brick walks can be set in sand using the same techniques as stone walks. For a more permanent installation, bricks can be installed in mortar over a concrete base. Once an area is excavated to an average depth of ten inches for a pedestrian walkway, 3/4" clear stone (or pea gravel—any free-draining material) is installed at an average depth of four inches. Over the top of this base, wood forms are fastened together to hold the wet concrete mix. Concrete is then mixed and poured into the forms. Once hardened, the forms can be removed and mortar can be mixed. The bricks can then be laid in mortar on top of the concrete base.

Concrete walks need an average base of four inches of clear stone beneath them for drainage. On top of this base, four inches of concrete will be laid (see "brick walks" above). Depending on how big an area is being paved, the concrete may need to be reinforced with steel, to increase its tensile strength, and wire mesh for stability. Any area larger than 400 square feet will need to be scored. Half-inch-deep saw cuts are intentionally made into the concrete to create weak points and ensure that, should the concrete crack, it will crack at pre-determined points. Scoring the concrete will take some thought, as the lines created can be a unique addition to the design.

Gravel walks are generally six inches deep for pedestrian walkways. At the bottom of the recessed area, a filter cloth or geotextile should be laid to prevent weeds from growing up through the gravel. Never use plastic underneath gravel. Because plastic doesn't breathe, moisture will collect and cause the path to heave with frosts and thaws.

The gravel can then be laid directly on top of the geotextile or filter cloth. A geotextile can also be a tremendous aid if you are in a clay soil environment; it can absorb much of the moisture and remove a situation where shifting might occur. Gravel paths often need edging, particularly if the stones are small, to keep them in place.

STEPS

Steps can be formal, orderly and symmetrical in nature. They can come in elegant pairs, curving up left and right to reach a terrace with a stone balustrade. Or steps can be informal, nothing more than a series of stepping-stones, weathered logs or grass treads that almost disappear into the landscape.

They can also be focal points, decorative features fitted out with statues, urns or even water running along-side. You may even design a fountain the middle of them. The only firm rule about step design is that the materials need to complement the house, as well as any nearby or adjacent walkways and walls that are within eyesight.

Six Essentials of Step Design

1. Calculate the ratio of risers to treads. In indoor spaces, most steps have risers that are between four and seven inches high. Treads are generally twelve inches deep. Outdoors, you'll want to keep to this formula if your stairway is in a well-traveled spot. The last thing you want to do while carrying groceries is worry about watching your feet. Generally, the risers of exterior steps are six inches in height and the treads are sixteen inches deep.

In outdoor areas where traffic is more leisurely, the measurements of both risers and treads can be altered to slow or speed up the pace of travel. Low risers and wide treads generally encourage faster steps. But when low risers are accompanied by treads that require two or three paces to cross, they slow down the pace of progress, making visitors pay more attention to their surroundings.

2. Calculate the number of steps. "It is a good rule to make the steps so easy that one can run up and down," wrote the great gardener Gertrude Jekyll, who looked as if she'd never run up—or down—a flight of steps. Nevertheless, her point is well taken. No one wants to be embarrassingly out of breath at any point on a garden stroll. A good stairway has anywhere from

Above: As these stairs by Dargan Landscape Architects demonstrate, steps not only allow people a route up or down to different areas but can also serve as a seating environment of sorts. **Opposite:** Stairs are the perfect platform for showcasing pots, plants and outdoor art. Utilize these elements to frame travel up and down the stairs.

Above: Here, a beautiful set of steps makes a concrete retaining wall, which creates usable terrace space on a sloping grade, into more than a strictly functional presence. **Opposite:** Stairs seem grander in appearance when framed by planted urns or pieces of art.

three to twelve steps. One or two lone steps are hard to see and possibly hazardous. More than twelve steps are hard to scale without a place to stop and breathe.

If you're faced with a long flight of steps, break it up with landings. On a steep grade, landings should come every three to eleven steps. Landings can either be functional places to pause or small terraces with seats and plantings.

3. Calculate the width of your steps. For a short climb, narrow steps are not a problem. But in most instances, steps should be at least four feet wide so that one person can be going up and another down without rubbing shoulders. The wider the steps, the more they become a place to stop, sit and enjoy the surroundings. When steps become wide enough for lounging, they cease to be merely functional and become a garden feature as well.

4. Decide on the course of your steps. Straight, curved or zigzag? The course should be dictated by the style and mood of your garden. Curved and zigzagging steps require a deliberate pace; it is hard to sprint up or down them. Straight steps are generally more functional and formal.

Steps that angle away from the path convey the feeling that you're taking a journey. Consider curving your steps around trees and planting beds to vary the view and add suspense to the journey

5. Choose your materials. For high-traffic areas, steps need to be sturdy. In less-traveled areas, materials such as boulders, gravel, grass and unsplit logs are options. Steps can be made with most of the same materials used for walkways, as well as with overlapping millstones and concrete treads.

Risers and treads can be made from different materials. For instance, pre-cast stones or cobblestones can be used for risers and interlocking stone for the treads, a good choice if interlocking stone is also used on walkways.

When choosing step materials, keep in mind the style of the house and any connecting walkways. It's best to repeat walkway materials in steps. If that's not possible, use materials with complementary colors and textures. Introducing too many different materials within a narrow area can be visually chaotic.

6. Integrate your steps into the landscape. The plain step edge is rarely attractive. Most stairs need to fit into a landscape by being united with a wall or blended into a slope cascading with plantings. In addition, steps can become part of the garden. Succulents and alpine plants can be grown on risers and low-growing plants encouraged to fill in the joints along the far edges of the treads.

To preserve the color of the hardscape material you've chosen for your walks, steps or driveway, consider a matte, gloss or semi-gloss silicone finish. This can easily be sprayed or rolled on with a tool similar to a paint roller. Not only will a silicone finish protect a driveway from oil, it will also keep hardscape materials from fading. The silicone finish should be applied one year after your hardscape has been installed. The wait allows natural brick and stone to release their efflorescence.

DRIVEWAYS

I have always felt that driveways demand special attention from a hardscaping point of view because they are such a critical element in the landscape. In poorly designed yards, vehicular areas sprawl over a large part of the property, creating a sector of your yard usable only as a parking lot. Since this is what people are accustomed to seeing, rethinking the driveway can dramatically change the experience of a landscape.

In all my design and construction classes, I ask my students to draft driveways that no one would ever want to drive on, treating the driveway as part of the landscape rather than an area to house our vehicles. After all, most residential driveways are empty of cars more than eighty percent of the time. This exercise helps to shift thinking away from an expanse of asphalt that interrupts the landscape and toward a solution that is integrated with the landscape.

I like to think of driveways as courtyards, rather than parking spots, and use them as a canvas for interesting paving materials. For one home that had a stucco finish, I poured a concrete driveway and matched the color and texture of the house's stucco by matching the stippled concrete finish on the ground plane. Then I added an inlay of limestone that echoed the angles of the roofline. When you add interesting materials or patterns to a driveway, I've found it stops feeling like a plain old driveway.

I pull my car into the garage as soon as I get home and encourage visitors to park on the street because I don't want them parking on my landscape. These habits contribute to curb appeal and no less significantly to the amount of livable space on the property.

Whether driveways are clumsy or graceful, they are never inexpensive. Their disproportionate size almost always incurs the largest cost in landscaping the home. But an investment in your driveway will pay off handsomely in terms of future resale value.

Opposite: Set against this stately house, the stamped asphalt looks like cobblestone. It makes the surface look more like a courtyard, giving the driveway an added level of interest. **Above:** A simple concrete driveway without pattern or texture can complement the natural stonework of the house façade.

Five Essentials of Driveway Design

1. **Consider the color of your materials.** Light gravel or black asphalt stands out in the landscape. To soften the look of asphalt, you can use it in conjunction with other materials, whether it be natural or interlocking stone. A concrete driveway will have to be at least four inches thick (six inches to eight inches for heavy trucks) and may glare unless colored or embedded with pebble aggregate.

2. **Allocate adequate space.** Remember that a parking space at the local mall is approximately nine feet wide by eighteen feet long. We are always bumping into the car next to us, and there never seems to be enough room to maneuver comfortably. So, when designing your driveway, think about having enough room for doors to open and circulation around the vehicle. If your proper-

ty is wide enough, you may want to consider a circular driveway or even a basketball half-court.

3. **Factor in water runoff.** Most driveways act as impermeable surfaces, even if they are not made of concrete or asphalt. The weight of cars will compact gravel and other permeable driveway materials, creating runoff issues. Depending on the size of your driveway and the slope of your land, you'll need to consider adding drainage leading to collection points. If your driveway is long, you may need to plan for a series of collection points to avoid a stream after a hard rain.

4. **Marry driveways and walks.** One of my pet peeves is a walkway that doesn't meet the driveway at a helpful point. Builders often try to save on expensive materials such as stone by designing walkways that take the shortest route from house to driveway. Often, this positions the walk too close to the house, leaving the person exiting his car with a short stroll to the start of the walkway.

I prefer to design the primary walkway to the front door so that it flows like a tributary right into the driveway. In other words, it actually runs alongside it for a short while and melds with the materials and the pattern of the driveway, rather than standing out as a separate element. Letting the walkway encroach on the driveway makes the former seem much larger and the latter much smaller.

In a more intricate driveway, re-route the front walkway to cut right into and through the driveway. On the other side, it turns back into a walkway again, in effect bridging the driveway and making the landscape dominant in the view.

5. **Give your driveway curb appeal.** To help locate the driveway for first-time visitors, make sure you have a distinctive mailbox or tree by the street. Stone pillars and a gate work nicely as well. Also make sure that when exiting the driveway, no plantings obscure the view of traffic.

Winding a driveway to traverse a steep grade not only makes the climb to the house more manageable, but also creates intrigue by only revealing a glimpse of the house at every turn.

When possible, plantings strategically placed along the driveway can hide, frame or highlight views. Try to hide the house until the last turn or approach.

Driveway Materials

Although more and more homeowners are looking for alternatives, asphalt remains a very good driveway material. It's inexpensive, durable, low maintenance and attractive. Its traditional color—black—actually works quite well in a landscape. The downside to asphalt is that it is malleable and on a hot summer day can become soft and scar. But in winter it helps snow melt because it absorbs heat.

Asphalt can be dressed up when used in concert with cobblestone, which is attractive on its own and useful for separating driveway and lawn. It can also be used with panels or inlays of a contrasting hardscaping material, such as decomposed granite. An asphalt driveway can be made less visually overwhelming by incorporating a soldier course, adding a border of hardscaping to frame the entire perimeter.

Concrete is another common driveway material that can be attractively used. Designer Michael Schneider colors his concrete with Davis colors, which are commonly used premixed tints (see www.daviscolors.com). Favorite hues include gray, salmon and taupe. "You can mix the color right into the cement mixer," says Schneider. He likes to do concrete driveways in two pours: one for solid panels and one for bands that will have aggregate added.

Concrete, like asphalt, requires a subsurface. Brick may be laid on a concrete base and mortared in order to withstand the weight of cars. Gravel and crushed rock, the least expensive driveway option, can be laid directly in a prepared depression of 4" to 5". As with walkways, filter cloth or geotextile should be laid to prevent weed growth. Gravel and loose rock come in a variety of colors, from soft white to barn red, and offer an attractive rustic look. They are best used with an edging, such as brick or stone, to prevent the stones from washing away or spreading.

4 BASICS

OF WALKWAYS, STEPS & DRIVEWAYS

1. *Understanding circulation is the key to functional accessways.* Before designing your walkways, steps or driveway, walk the grounds around your home to get a feel for the dominant paths of travel, as well as where your core garden elements should be positioned.

2. *Decide on whether your path is a primary, secondary and tertiary means of access.* Each type of path has a different set of design parameters, including the types of materials that are appropriate.

3. *Materials for accessways should integrate not only with the house and outdoor surroundings, but also with other accessways.* Make sure to look at projected materials next to nearby walkways, steps and driveways.

4. *Use restraint.* Don't forget that your landscape is a natural environment. Be creative and create appropriate accessways without overdoing it.

If you're designing a driveway from scratch, there are several new materials that won't cost appreciably more than baseline paving. Cobblestone is widely used for driveways now, since it can be manufactured inexpensively from interlocking stone to give a very good imitation of aged granite. The material is durable and designer-friendly. I like to drill lights directly into the cobble set to create evening interest.

I use a lot of interlocking pavers when I want to give a driveway the feeling of a courtyard. Interlocking pavers, which can be dry laid, lend themselves nicely to pattern. I've designed driveways with geometric inlays, swirls of patterns, or even a centerpiece of four arches. A versatile system called paver quilting is rapidly gaining popularity. This is the use of many different pre-cast products together to create a uniform walkway, patio or driveway. All components in this system are pre-matched, enabling the homeowner to choose among numerous materials and mix them together in a larger expanse of hardscape. It is virtually impossible to make a mistake using this system.

The best material for a driveway is one that suits your budget and matches the aesthetics of the house. And if you can't afford the most appropriate option, be creative. For example, if you have stone detailing on your house and can't afford a stone driveway, perhaps you can work stone patterning around the edge of the driveway.

No matter what materials you choose for walkways, stairs or driveways, always consult a professional when deciding the installation technique. You will get a longer life out of landscape investment and a higher rate of return upon resale.

Opposite: Make sure the material you choose for your driveway complements the style of your home. Here, a gravel driveway is what you would expect at a country estate set in a wooded rural environment.
Above: Interlocking stone bordered by concrete is a beautiful contemporary design that is gaining popularity.

WOOD

Wood is found in nearly every landscape design. It may be a prominent feature, such as a gate, pergola, fence, deck, trellis, gazebo, or arbor; or it may be simply a part of the construction process, such as bracing and formwork for concrete. Wood is a popular choice for many hardscaping applications largely because of its warmth and visual appeal. It can be fancy or rustic, has sturdy and homey connotations, and suits almost any style of surroundings. Nonetheless, deciding to use wood means limited options and hard choices because most wood degrades fast and rots easily with exposure to sun and rain.

There are ways to retard rotting. Where wood comes in contact with the ground, you should use chromated copper arsenate (CCA) to help preserve the wood and protect it from water damage. This is the preferred sealing agent because it uses waterborne preservatives, is non-oily and odorless. There is no problem of leaching into the ground because it is neither oil-based nor toxic.

Types of Wood

Three types of wood are used in landscaping: lumber, plywood and timbers. Lumber is up to 5" thick: 1" x 1", 1" x 2", 2" x 2", 2" x 4", etc. Anything over 5" is considered timber. Plywood is made up of very thin sheets of wood glued together, with the grain in each sheet running in opposite directions for stability. The applications for plywood are mostly limited to architectural features (benches, storage areas, etc.) and roofing, while lumber and timber are used for numerous applications in the landscape. Timber is appropriate primarily for retaining walls, stairs and some fences; lumber will be used in virtually any wood construction.

1.

2.

3.

1. Wood adds softness to outdoor areas. In shape and color, it is a versatile material becuase it can be cut to specification and painted or stained. 2. Very intricate deck designs are possible with wood. This sunburst was labor-intensive but a great solution to cover the garage.

3. Get creative with your fence designs and look for new ideas. Research woods that can last over time in your climate zone.

4.

5.

6.

When ordering lumber, the dimensions are always thickness by width by length (i.e., a 2" x 4" x 10' will be 2" thick by 4" wide by 10' long.) But bear in mind: Wood is measured in its rough cut form, before the lumberyard has shaved off slivers to smooth the edges and then dried it, which will traditionally shrink the wood by 12%. So the dimensions for thickness and width will always be approximately 3/8" smaller than advertised. A 2" x 4", for example, is actually about 1 5/8" x 3 5/8".

PROS
1. It's lightweight, easy to move and doesn't require machinery to put it into place.
2. It's very versatile: You can use it on the ground plane, on the vertical plane or overhead.
3. It will accept different finishes, from translucent stains to opaque paints.
4. From a maintenance standpoint, you can easily replace warped or rotted boards.
5. You can pre-build sections in a shop, such as portions of a fence.

CONS
1. Unless treated, it can catch fire.
2. Unless treated, it can rot and decay.
3. The joints where two pieces come together are an inherent weak point structurally.
4. It can be expensive, especially grade A cedar and hardwoods.
5. It will wear with extended use.

4. These large timbers support the roof and are visually intruiging. Together with the textured, tongue-and-groove ceiling and lattice panels, this space is proof that wood can be both functional and interesting. **5.** Plywood is used to form and shape concrete. It is put in place, oiled, then removed once the concrete has been poured and cured. **6.** Decks are typically built with lumber that measures 2" x 4", 4" x 6", or 2"x 8". Try using clips beneath the boards, rather than nails or screws, to secure lumber.

Types of Lumber

The following groupings, arranged from least expensive to most expensive, will give you a basic understanding of the lumber that may be appropriate for your job.

PRESSURE-TREATED SOFTWOODS

Pressure-treated lumber, usually softwoods such as pine or spruce, is by far the most commonly used wood for hardscaping. This material, which is chemically treated to resist the elements, has the advantage of being plentiful and cheap. For years, consumers have believed that its only disadvantage is the vaguely greenish discoloration introduced by processing board lengths, but now there's a growing concern that processing also poses an environmental hazard. You may want to check with your local building department to see if there are any issues with respect to use of pressure-treated lumber in your community. Because pine and spruce need to be chemically treated to resist the elements, a simple nail hole or saw cut, if left untreated, will encourage rot and decay. So make sure to treat all the marks you've made to your pressure-treated lumber during installation with pentachlorophenol, which can be found at any building supply store or lumberyard.

PROS
1. It's the most inexpensive form of lumber available.
2. It's easy to find.
3. It's weather resistant.

CONS
1. It may pose an environmental hazard.
2. It can discolor in the sun.
3. If all cuts and scars in the wood are not chemically treated, it will rot.
4. Because the grains are obscured, you can't stain it effectively.

1.

2.

3.

1. Pressure-treated lumber is usually very easy to find. Make sure to hand-pick the lumber to ensure that you are selecting straight boards, without splits and warps. 2. Pressure-treated wood has a green tinge when purchased; that's the protective layer that prevents rot. To ensure the longevity of your new deck or railing, use a sealant on any cuts you make in the wood.
3. Virtually any type of wood available in cedar is also available in pressure-treated lumber, including these pre-fabricated lattice panels. Normally, you can purchase large sections of these panels, cutting down on construction time.

CONSTRUCTION GRADE CEDAR

Construction grade cedar is the higher-end alternative to pressure-treated lumber, usually twice the cost. Its resistance to moisture, UV rays and insects that bore into the wood comes naturally, and cedar significantly outperforms the chemically treated competition. Often, I will suggest using pressure-treated lumber for the structural support of the deck and cedar for the decking itself. This is the most widely used and widely available form of lumber.

PROS
1. It's widely available.
2. It will accept a finish of stain or paint.
3. You can see the actual grains in it.

CONS
1. It may be full of knots, which may pop out over time.
2. It may warp or split.
3. The color is not uniform: Some pieces may be darker than others.

4.

5.

6.

4. The overhead canopy here is made from tongue-and-groove cedar boards, while the deck and column are made from construction grade cedar. The double Adirondack chairs/table in the foreground is weathered pine. When these items weather together, the grays should match. 5. Painting or staining wood is beneficial as it protects the wood from future decay or rot, and you can choose colors or shades that work best with the exterior of your home. 6. Construction grade cedar is the most common type of cedar found in landscapes. If left untreated, the color will change over time to a dull gray.

LAMINATED TIMBERS

Laminated timbers is a third alternative. This material is produced by gluing together individual pieces of wood that have been stripped down from larger pieces of lumber. This product is not to be confused with Glulam (glued-laminated timbers); this is a structural timber used predominately for interior structural applications. Laminated timbers are used within the landscape primarily for larger beam construction and archways. This process is very time consuming, but the end results are worth the effort. Wonderful large scale beams and archways can be created that will bear heavy loads and the crushing power of vines such as wisteria. The final look of a laminated timber pergola or archway will immediately stand out as a focal point and conversation piece in your landscape.

PROS

1. The average length of spans of wood can be greatly increased without increasing the bulk.
2. Because this is something that is normally built off site and then installed on a property, the elements of nature do not affect its construction; these structures can be built indoors, in rain or snow.
3. The building process allows curves to be built into the wood structure without introducing numerous joints.

CONS

1. It is a costly alternative because of the intense labor required to assemble it.
2. If the correct glues are not used or there are impurities within the glues, there is the potential for de-lamination in certain weather conditions.
3. Some find the final layering appearance of the lamination process unsightly and will paint the finished product rather than use a clear stain.

1.

2.

1. Old barn beams predate laminated timbers. Due to the high cost of obtaining large or oversized timbers like these today, they tend to be cost prohibitive. However, resourceful buyers can actually purchase the timber from ruined barns or farmhouses.

2. Laminating timbers allows the construction of larger load-bearing timbers at a fraction of the cost of steel or solid timbers. They can be used in the landscape as load-bearing members or have more of a decorative purpose like holding up a weaving vine.

NON-PRESSURE-TREATED SOFTWOODS

Other softwoods, such as redwood, Douglas fir, spruce and Jack pine, are further alternatives. Non-pressure-treated softwoods, of course, won't have the same weather resistance as pressure-treated varieties, though because they are less expensive, they may be useful in sheltered areas or as structural wood. Douglas fir is among the hardest of the softwoods and weathers quite well. It is also the heaviest softwood. Because of its density, it will withstand warping and splitting. Redwood is also highly resistant to decay and comes in a color range from mahogany to gray. It's heavier than cedar, lighter than fir.

PROS

1. They can be visually stunning.
2. Compared with hardwoods, they are relatively inexpensive.
3. They grow faster than hardwood and are more readily available.
4. They come in a wide variety of colors.
5. If it is from the heartwood (center of the tree), it is resistant to decay.
6. There's little shrinkage.

CONS

1. The sapwood (from the outside of the tree) is prone to rot and decay.
2. Some softwoods, such as spruce, don't take stains as well as others.
3. Some of the firs are not very durable and will decay easily.
4. When in regular contact with ground moisture, they'll rot.
5. They are prone to splitting and warping.

3.

3. Laminated timbers are more commonly used to form curved pergolas or arches. These slivers of wood are placed into a form, and each sliver is glued to the next and clamped together. A pergola like the one featured here may have up to 25 layers of wood glued together before it is cut, sanded and then painted in place.

GRADE A CEDAR

Grade A, knot-free clear cedar is an almost grainless wood in fairly good supply. Structurally and aesthetically, it is exceptional, though it is expensive and can be two to three times the cost of lower end cedars, as much as five times the cost of pressure-treated lumber. Still, many homeowners are beginning to understand that the cost of purchase should be weighed against the cost of upkeep for less expensive materials.

PROS

1. It's free of knots.
2. The coloring is consistent throughout.
3. There's very little warping and splitting.
4. It's visually beautiful and weathers gracefully.

CONS

1. It's expensive.
2. It's not widely available.

1.

2.

3.

1. Grade A cedar is very expensive and hard to find in large quantities. But if your budget allows, select this material—chances are it will outlive you. This type of cedar can be used in traditional ways or curved to form vertical lattice features. 2. Teak furniture has long been revered as the king of exterior furniture because of its density and longevity. This type of garden furniture will cost more but is often an heirloom that can be handed down. 3. When purchasing raw wood or wood furniture, always check for any splitting or warping and discard these pieces. Look for knot-free wood and clarity of the wood grain.

4.

5.

6.

DENSE HARDWOODS

A variety of dense hardwoods, such as Brazilian hardwood, mahogany, oak and teak, are also being marketed today. These are considered "exotics" and are therefore costly alternatives. The installation is also more expensive than either pressure-treated lumber or cedar, as the density of the wood requires extra time to assemble. With Brazilian wood, for example, you may need to pre-drill your nail holes. It is, however, extremely strong and resistant to rot. Built right, a hardwood deck could last for centuries. Because of the cost, though, most people use these sorts of dense hardwoods for interior or sheltered applications or, most commonly, for garden furniture that can be brought in out of the rain.

PROS

1. They're visually stunning and often the best choice for garden furniture.
2. They're structurally quite sound and hard.
3. There's very little warping or splitting.
4. They will take virtually any type of finish. When stained, the beauty of the grains is magnified.
5. There are a wide variety of grains, from maple (virtually no grains) to oak (a great deal of grains).
6. They come in a wide range of shades, from very light to dark browns.

CONS

1. Hardwoods are the most expensive lumber, and outside usage is often cost prohibitive.
2. They're not widely available, and large quantities must be ordered in advance.
3. Because they are so hard, more labor is required for installation.

4. Modern designs for outdoor furniture now come in all shapes and forms. The design of this teak outdoor bar, complete with built-in sink, cutting board and cupboards, is appropriate for a wood deck. **5.** There is no end to what you can create in teak. Likely, you won't see many garbage containers in a patio setting, but when they are as nice as this one and blend in with your furniture, you can place a few in your entertainment area. **6.** Teak dining tables come in unique designs. Most are flexible and designed to expand for large groups and retract for smaller ones.

CHAPTER 5

WATERSCAPES
FOUNTAINS, PONDS, POOLS & WATERFALLS

There are hundreds of reasons to add water features to your yard. They stimulate the senses and add light, movement and dynamics to the landscape; they beckon us outside to watch, listen, splash or be alone with our

thoughts; they offer us places for recreation and relaxation. But the simplest reason is that water makes a landscape come alive in the most appealing way.

How you choose to incorporate water into your landscape depends on whether you want to venture into the water—i.e., swim, sit in a Jacuzzi, lounge in a grotto beneath a waterfall—or simply admire it via a fountain, pond or reflecting pool. Do you want a habitat for humans or a habitat for water plants and fish? Would you rather experience the quiet trickle of a fountain or the rush of a waterfall?

Whether you opt for an elaborate pool or a simple birdbath, water is critical in making a landscape both beautiful to look at and enjoyable to experience. Anyone who has ever experienced a yard before and after the addition of a fountain, pond or pool understands how water draws us to it. I've seen backyards that go completely unused until a pond or pool has been added, and then suddenly they become a central gathering place. Because of this—as well as the impact a good water feature will have on your property values—you should view water elements as important investments, both financially and personally.

FOUNTAINS

The simplest way to enhance your property with the sound and movement of water is by installing a fountain.

Because it draws attention to itself with anything from a pleasant trickling to a dramatic spray of water, a fountain is a natural focal point. It is generally positioned along an important axis—a sightline from the front or back door, perhaps, or a central path from the terrace to the rose garden. But fountains can also have a quieter role. They can be set into terraces to provide a soothing backdrop to parties or incorporated into front walkways to screen out street noise and create a feeling of sanctuary.

Fountain styles range from simple faucets that send water trickling down a wall to three-tiered extravaganzas with dolphins and nymphs. Similarly, fountain nozzles come in an astonishing array. Whether you want a half-dozen jets arching up six feet in the air or just a simple bubbler, there's an option for you. I would only caution you to think carefully about how your fountain will fit with its surroundings. If you live on a crowded suburban street, for example, a fierce lion's head spewing streams of water on your front lawn may give your neighbors pause.

In considering what style and type of fountain to install, your first consideration should be the role a fountain will play in your landscape. Here are some factors to consider:

- Will your fountain be viewed from all sides or from one?
- Will it punctuate a path and or will it be part of a sitting area?

Opposite: Water is a welcome feature in any landscape. It adds an element of calm and serenity to the environment and can be used for a variety of activities, from swimming to simply viewing.

One of the easiest ways to combine hardscape and water is to create a water wall, with water flowing down the side of the wall. I've designed a three-foot horizontal slit in a concrete wall that edges a dining area and then turned that section into a mini water wall. The water is collected in a rock-filled basin, and the pipe that re-circulates the water is hidden behind the wall. It is an enchanting sight.

- How large do you want the sprays to be?
- How many different layers of sprays or nozzles do you want?
- At what angle should the jets be set?
- How wide should the basin or pond be?
- How much noise should the fountain generate?
- What will your fountain look like in winter when the water is turned off?

When using shooting sprays, the nozzles determine the water pattern, and the height of the spray determines the size of the basin or pond you will need. As a general rule, the basin or pond needs to be twice as wide as the height of the spray in order to prevent your fountain from splashing guests and watering walkways. Thus, if you have one center column of water shooting straight up four feet, you will need a basin or pool that is at least eight feet in diameter.

Simple Fountain Ideas

Fountains don't have to be grand. Less is often more, so be creative. If you find a set of well-shaped boulders, you can drill holes in them, run a pipe through, position a pump and a lower basin underneath and let the water brim and cascade down the sides of the boulders. I've even created a fountain by mounting a watering can to a wall. A hose attached to it serves as a water source, and a pump hidden in a collecting basin re-circulates it.

Landscape architect Joan Honeyman turns beautiful oversized concrete urns from Lunaform (www.lunaform.com) into gently trickling fountains using the same principle. Water overflows down the sides of the urns into a basin covered with pebbles and rocks. A pump, hidden among the rocks, re-circulates the water. In the winter, when the fountain is turned off, the urn is still a beautiful focal point. She likes to position these by driveways or at the entrance to screen out street noise and add a soothing backdrop to conversation.

Left: A large garden is not required for water features. In fact, for a re-circulating water feature, all you need is a bit of wall space. **Opposite:** Drama definitely plays a role in water features. Think about how compelling a water feature would be in your outdoor space, as this fountain is here.

PONDS

If you don't have a natural spring or stream running through your property, a pond can nonetheless be yours relatively simply. All you have to do is dig a hole, add a liner, then add water. At your garden store, you'll discover pumps that not only re-circulate water but also filter it. With the right equipment, you can avoid some or a lot of regular maintenance. Of course, you'll likely need to skim leaves in the fall and occasionally thin water plants that may grow too densely. And fish, if you have them, will need to be taken inside during the winter or kept warm with a submersible heater.

These minor chores are a small price to pay for the addition of a pond. However, be sure to think through all contingencies, and consult with professionals before you install one. A pond is not only a habitat for the plants and animals you want to see there, it's also one for those you don't. Deer, geese and any number of wild animals in the area may be as attracted to the pond as you are. Ponds can also create environments for weeds, and you don't want to see your pond turn into a swamp.

Three Ways to Build a Pond

Ponds with preformed liners. Perhaps you've seen these preformed plastic or Fiberglas liners at home building stores or garden centers. They are attractively shaped and ready to be strapped to the roof of your car. They are appealing in that they take all the guesswork out of pond design. On the other hand, what you see is what you get. There's no chance of altering the shape to suit that little bend in the landscape you forgot about. They are also difficult to combine with waterfalls because it's hard to build up a natural looking rise for the waterfall and also difficult to hide the water pump.

Still, preformed liners are relatively easy to install. You simply dig a big hole and pop them in. The trick is

Above: Man-made ponds can be created where a landscape lacks a natural stream or spring. Here, strategically placed stepping-stones and plants help make the water more inviting to viewers.

Opposite: As this image demonstrates, building steps down into a pond creates a natural area for seating. Viewers can experience the elements of this pond close-up, as well as hear its soothing sounds.

making sure they're level so that water won't spill out or look awkward. Their decided advantage is their sturdiness. Kids can walk in them. Rocks can be tossed in them. And they are designed to avoid cracking and leaks. Also, preformed pools support themselves and can therefore be used aboveground on a deck or terrace.

Ponds with rubber liners. As a liner, rubber is an excellent material because it can be formed in any shape. For instance, if you start digging your pond and realize you'd like to have it wider in the sunshine and narrower in the shade, you can alter it. Rubber liners come in big sheets or on big rolls. Rather like buying fabric by the yard, you buy a piece of liner in the size you want.

The downside to rubber liners is that they can spring a leak if you're not careful. To protect them from any rocks that might be in the soil, lay a three-inch base of sand. As an additional barrier, it's a good idea to add a filter cloth or geotextile. When installing the liner, only walk on it in stocking feet. And don't use any sharp tools in its vicinity. This may seem obvious, but on more than one occasion, I've caught my crew spreading pebbles across the bottom with a rake. It's an easy mistake to make. One more thing: If rocks or pebbles are used to line the pond bottom or ledges you've created, they need to be rounded.

Despite all these warnings, rubber-lined ponds are wonderful. Carefully installed, they can last indefinitely. Over the 20 years I've had my business, I've had only one spring a leak. While annoying, a leak is not tragic; it can be patched with a rubber weld, a job that involves high heat and is best left to a pond expert.

Ponds with concrete liners. Like rubber, concrete can be used for ponds of virtually any size and shape. The primary difference between the two materials is cost. It's expensive and labor-intensive to install a concrete shell, which requires a series of forms and pours.

But concrete has distinct advantages. It can be designed to a more precise shape, which is useful if you're planning a formal rectangular pond, perhaps one that doubles as a reflecting pool. Concrete is also versatile, in that stone or tile can be mortared to it, either as a liner for the pond or a coping. This adds to the price of a pond but also to its beauty.

Essentials of Pond Design

Decide on the purpose. Do you want a pond to be a water feature or a place for wading? Will it be a focal point, part of a sanctuary or a private area next to a bench or hammock? Do you want to leave the water clear, or do you want to add fish and aquatic plants? Do you want a still pool that reflects the trees and sky, or do you want to add jets or bubbler heads so that you create noise and movement?

Decide on the shape and style. As I've mentioned many times, any hardscape feature needs to relate to the architecture of the house. If your house is formal, a rectangular or round reflecting pool would be more appropriate than a freeform pond surrounded by boulders with a trickling waterfall. Remember that if a pond is far enough away from your house, you have license to experiment with a different and perhaps more rustic style.

Decide on the dimensions—and when in doubt,

Concrete is a good choice for pond basin material, as its versatility allows you to form any shape that you desire.

think big. A preformed liner in a store can look huge. In your yard, it may be just the opposite. I've found that people generally fail to think big enough when it comes to ponds, even if they carefully plot them on paper as we discussed in Chapter 1, *Designing Outdoor Spaces.* Which is why it's important to spread a tarp or take a garden hose and mark where your pond will be. Be sure to view your marked area from many points in your yard—and from first- and second-floor windows that will benefit from a view.

Decide on depth. Ponds can be shallower than most people think. Two-and-a-half feet is a perfectly good depth. If the pond has a black liner, it will look bottomless. A shallow pond may let you avoid the need for safety fencing, which is required around all swimming pools and ponds of a certain depth. Before you start your design process, be sure to check your local building codes.

Decide how to edge your pond. The edges of preformed and rubber liners need to be hidden and in some way incorporated with the landscape. Most often this is accomplished by adding a border of rocks and plants that gives the illusion the pond always existed in the landscape. Growing plants in the pond will further blur the line between yard and pond. Concrete ponds can likewise be given a naturalistic edging. But they also offer the option for formal copings of mortared stone and tile.

Pond Design Dos and Don'ts

Don't site a pond in a low area of your lawn, even though it would seem like the most natural location. You don't want water draining into your pond and creating maintenance problems. Also, be sure to grade the area around the pond so water will flow away. This is especially important if you have fish, since lawn fertilizers and garden chemicals are toxic to fish.

Don't plunk ponds in the middle of your lawn. Though that may be the simplest and most obvious place

While today's bio-filters eliminate the need for adding chemicals and can make pond water virtually maintenance-free, you'll need to consider the following:

- *If you have fish, how will you feed them?* This won't be an issue if you set up a balanced pond ecosystem with plants.
- *What will you do with fish in the winter?* They'll need to be brought inside and established in an indoor aquarium, or else your pond will need to be heated with a submersible heater.
- *Will you shut down your pond in winter months?* If water is left in the pipes, they can freeze and crack, so you should have them dried with a sort of large hair dryer. Though you can do this yourself, often it is a job for a professional.
- *Do you have trees that will shed leaves and flowers onto your pond?* Ponds are best sited away from deciduous trees. Tannins from leaves can deplete the water's oxygen level, while roots can damage liners, especially rubber ones. If tree roots are unavoidable, try a partially raised pond. In the fall, a net can also be used to catch leaves.
- *How will unwanted plants and animals respond to your pond?* Again, talk to a garden or landscape expert to find out if migrating geese will descend upon your pond, or if it could suddenly sprout exotic flora you hadn't planned on.

to put a pond, it is something of a cliché. Ponds should be sited where they can be enjoyed, either in a quiet spot where you like to retreat or somewhere close to the house.

Do incorporate ponds into existing features. Highlight a wall or steps by building a raised pond next to it. Build a pond into a terrace or paved areas. Beautifully edged with plants, a terrace pond will add character to your entertaining area.

Don't despair if you live in a small space. Small properties are just as amenable to water features as larger ones, and small installations can be quite economical. A pond can expand the look and feel of your yard. In a confined space, this is one of the best ways to introduce variety into the landscape. If you live in an apartment, a preformed liner will let you have a small rooftop or balcony pond. (Again, check building codes and consult engineers to see if weight is an issue.)

Don't let water stagnate. Still water is a breeding ground for mosquitoes. If you don't have a waterfall, add a bubbler or spray jets to create motion and movement in the water.

Do plan for the unexpected. Whatever you think your pond installation will take in terms of cost and labor, double it. No matter how carefully you design a pond or a waterfall on paper, it's hard to get that third dimension right, especially with naturalistic ponds, which are dependent on unique materials. You might find rocks for the edging that are particularly beautiful but a bit too large. Figuring out how to alter the shape or slope of a pond to work them in will add expense. Or perhaps you find a boulder with fossils in it that you want to feature. Pond design is an art, and no matter how well you plan ahead, there are decisions that can only be made on-site.

The designers of this water feature used the natural topography of the land to place the pond and waterfall in the best locations. Here, the waterfall has been placed at the natural crest of the garden.

Though aquatic plants need a fair amount of light, fish do not like to bask in sunny water. Thus, it is essential to design a fish pond with varying depths and little caves that will be cool and afford hiding places from any predators. This is especially important if your yard is visited by wildlife. Perhaps the most persistent predators are raccoons, who fortunately hate to swim. If you install a shallow underwater ledge followed by a deep plunge, raccoons won't go farther than the ledge, and fish will have a safe place to hide.

SWIMMING POOLS

I've had clients add swimming pools to back yards even when they don't swim. The reason? Swimming pools are natural gathering places. Everyone loves to sit beside water and, if the hardscape permits, host poolside dinner parties. What makes an appealing pool? Here are some factors to consider:

• **Style.** A pool should suit the architecture of your house. If your house is Victorian, you might want a classic formal pool surrounded by elaborately patterned paving. If your house is modern, you might want a dramatic deck cantilevered over a geometric concrete pool. On the other hand, if your pool is remote from your house, you have more license to experiment with a different style.

• **Purpose.** If your pool is strictly for exercise, make it longer rather than wider. If it's going to be used for casual dips and cooling off, make it hospitably wide and avoid sharp angles. If it's primarily a setting for formal dinners and garden parties, you might want to add jets to turn it into a nighttime fountain.

• **Location.** Pool contractors love to place pools right in the center of a yard, which limits your ability to create garden rooms in the rest of the property. If you have enough space, a pool should be some distance from the house, inviting you to wander through the garden.

• **Shade.** Siting a pool too close to large trees will leave you perpetually skimming leaves. But you'll probably want some shade on the patio surrounding your pool. Umbrellas can do the trick; so can an awning or a pergola covered with flowering vines.

• **Access.** Most families who have children want pools with access on four sides. But pools can look wonderful blended with flower or herb gardens on one or more sides.

Opposite: As this free-form pool illustrates, pools can dominate a landscape. Even so, its style and shape help it fit into its natural setting. **Above:** Pools can also be designed to blend into the background. To reduce the amount of fill that had to be removed, the designers raised this pool above the existing grade and installed stairs and a retaining wall. This can help if machine access is an issue.

• **Fencing.** Your local building codes will specify that a pool must be surrounded by a fence of a certain height and fitted with locked gates. Fencing can surround the entire back yard. But if small children are involved, it's advisable to fence the immediate pool area. A fence that meets code may not be attractive but it can be faced with lattice and covered with climbing vines. Or hedges or

trees can be planted in front of it. (For more ideas see Chapter 3, *Enclosure*.)

• **Privacy.** A safety fence ensures only limited privacy. Neighbors may still be able to look out from their second floor bedrooms and observe you in your Speedo. The best way to make a pool private is to plant trees at the perimeter of the pool area or at the perimeter of your property.

• **Noise.** Keep in mind that sound travels over water, and poolside laughter will definitely be heard by nearby neighbors. Again, softscape may be the answer; shrubs can muffle sound.

• **Diving.** With liability such an issue, I rarely design pools with diving boards any more. Because diving boards are spring-loaded, people can easily have accidents. A safer solution is a diving rock. A small boulder or a series of multi-sized boulders can be placed at the edge of the pool.

• **Stairs.** For safety, you'll need ladders in the deep end. In the shallow end, you'll want steps for wading into the pool. If you can, extend the perimeter of the pool to make room for the steps. If the steps are set in their own arc, they will be out of the way of the swimming area, and swimmers won't end up with stubbed toes or grazed arms.

• **Materials.** Like ponds, pools can be made with vinyl or Fiberglas liners, or they can be made with sprayed gunite, a form of concrete with added plasticity. Until recently, preformed liners with their faux tile patterns on the side were less aesthetically appealing. But today vinyl liners are very appealing. They can even be paired with mortared stone or tile borders and copings. Their clear advantage is that they are far less expensive than a concrete pool and may free up a sizable chunk of the budget for a Jacuzzi or another amenity. One disadvantage: It's tricky to make a waterfall look natural with a preformed liner.

Previous Page: When designing pools close to the home, pay careful attention to how your materials integrate with those of the house.
Left: Be sure to use large changes in a grade to your advantage. This upper level hot tub cascades into a swimming pool, and the natural stone staircase wades into water—a great use of existing grade changes.

The Ultimate Swimming Pool

If you want to go all out, consider the following:

• *Negative edge or infinity pools are increasingly popular.* This type of pool has one edge (usually running the full length of the pool) that seems to disappear into the horizon. In reality, the water at that edge is cascading over a two- to four-inch-thick tempered glass wall into a

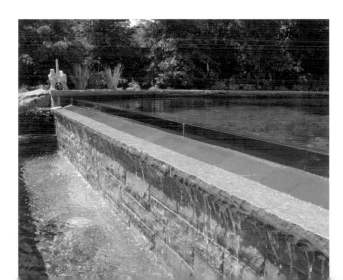

hidden gutter. From there, the water is pumped back into the pool and recirculated. The effect works best if the infinity edge of the pool leads away from the house toward another body of water—i.e., a lake, a river, the ocean. But landscape architect Michael Schneider has used an infinity edge when the view is simply of a lawn beyond. "The trick is not to put any planting on the edge of lawn," he explains. "You want a sweeping, uninterrupted view."

• For a small property, try a lap or plunge pool. The former can be designed as a formal reflecting pool so it is a proper garden feature. It need not be very deep or wide—four feet in depth and width is sufficient. A plunge pool, on the other hand, is small but deep. Rather like a large hot tub, they're usually eight or nine feet deep and ten or twelve feet in diameter. They can be designed with

Above: Water from a negative edge or infinity pool appears to fall gracefully into the landscape beyond. This type of swimming pool is very effective when combined with a black bottom. **Left:** The special effect of a negative edge pool is to have the water disappear seamlessly over an edge, heat it, then filter and recirculate it to the upper level.

a seating shelf and outfitted with jets that blast water at you. Swim furiously toward the jets, and you'll simply be swimming in place, getting a very hearty workout. Jets can be installed in larger pools, though the added size makes the setup more costly.

• *A hot tub can have a sculpture or fountain at its center,* tinted dark to conceal the fixtures. So too a pool can double as a fountain if you install jets on its floor that shoot sprays of water three or more feet above the pool surface. The jets can be on a timer with or without a manual override. At night, they can switch on along with the lighting.

• *Build a grotto under a waterfall.* Behind the sheet of water coming down the waterfall, you can design a little cave with a seating shelf. Swim through the water, and you can be rewarded with a bar. Anything is possible.

• *Add a fountain.* A sculpture can send water cascading down into your pool, creating a musical backdrop. Or jets can be installed at the bottom of the swimming pool to send water shooting up three or so feet above the surface. This is a wonderful way to give a pool a second use, especially at night when lighting can turn the fountain sprays into a dramatic focal point.

Top: Swimming pool designs are limited only by your imagination. Make sure to incorporate the basics of design: elements, principles and form composition. **Bottom:** Pool houses should integrate with the pool landscape. This one is architecturally significant, consistent with the pool hardscape and offers more than just shelter.

The Pool House

More and more, I'm being asked to design not just pools but pool houses—cabanas complete with changing rooms, wet bars, kitchens, wood pizza ovens, fireplaces, outdoor showers, you name it. It's an inviting challenge, and I like to start with a cooking pavilion—a small veranda where a grill, built into a counter, faces the patio. (A host standing at a grill should always look toward his or her guests.) Whenever possible, I make grills focal points, partly because they are the heart of a party and partly because freestanding grills never have enough room for plates and platters. When a grill is built into a counter fitted out with bar stools, guests can chat as the chicken grills.

The pool house also has a number of functional purposes, keeping wet swimsuits and wet feet out of the main house. It also eliminates the inevitable extra trip back to the house for ice or a serving spoon during par-

Outdoor kitchens can include refrigerators, sinks, grills and storage spaces. The cabana that houses the kitchen might also include changing rooms, washrooms, showers, storage and pool equipment.

ties. Not only that, a pool house is a practical place to store off-season pool furniture. I like to include a small room—six by eight feet is a good size—for stowing pool furniture off-season. The pool heater and filter can also be hidden in this room.

A few extra square feet could also be guest quarters—the options are limited only by your imagination and budget. Just be sure to consider the scale and style of the pool when designing surrounding structures so that they work together to make a single design statement. The design of the cabana is a prime opportunity to establish continuity between pool, home and landscape.

Spa Design

Whirlpools are social places. I like to design them adjacent to swimming pools so that water can flow from one to another and recirculate through both. Normally, a whirlpool is walled off from the main pool so the jets can stir up the water. Even so, a good pool designer can creatively place the spa within the swimming pool. From a distance, you won't see the jets at all.

Though it is attractive to have a seamless whirlpool and swimming pool, a sociable alternative is to design whirlpools so that they are 18" higher than the main pool. That way guests can sit around the edge of the pool and talk to those who are relaxing within. If a whirlpool is higher, it can be designed with a Plexiglas wall. Water can cascade over it, creating the same infinity edge that is used in swimming pools (see above).

Hardscaping for Swimming Pools

As much as the actual design of a swimming pool, the hardscaping also determines the look. We've come a long way from the old concrete patios. Today stone, interlocking pavers and a variety of other materials are used poolside. I like to extend the paving material right up to the edge of the pool so that it has an elegant, seamless look.

Coping stones, the edging around a pool, can have two finishes, with ends that are either bull-nosed (sloping) or square. Either way, I like to extend the coping so it has a 1" – 2" overhang. Since pools are in full sun, this normally creates a shadow and adds an elegant finish. Fiber-optic lighting can also be installed under the coping. Various colors are available, though I prefer simple white.

Here, a stone hot tub overlooks a wooded valley. Consider what types of paving material would be appropriate for this type of garden pool setting. Natural stone and wood are popular choices that work well here.

How much hardscaping do you need around a pool? If you want just a walkway, you'll need at least three feet of paving. If you anticipate sunbathing, you'll need at least eight feet of paving to accommodate lounging and traffic.

Hardscaping around a pool can essentially be treated as a terrace (see Chapter 2, *Rooms with a View*) and can even include planting pockets at the water's edge to create a natural look. Keep in mind that you'll need adequate drainage for your planting pockets. And you won't want to cultivate any plants that have aggressive root systems that might damage pool walls.

Top: Always consider circulation around furniture when designing the final size of your patio. Here, a random rectangular flagstone patio is complemented by a modular, clay brick soldier course. **Right:** Today's technological advances allow interlocking stone to be installed as the pool coping right to the water's edge.

Waterfalls

One way to add interest to a pond or swimming pool is to create a recirculating waterfall. In a perfect world, the water would fall from a raised area that exists on your property. Since the world is rarely perfect, most waterfalls need to be built into a bermed or built-up area that appears gradual. In designer terms, this is called feathering the grade.

The scale and proportion of the waterfall should be determined by the setting. Though it's possible to put a 20-foot-high waterfall in most any yard, it is not always possible to make it look as if it belongs there.

Since a waterfall is an excellent focal point, its position on your pond or pool should be considered in relation to the central axes and sight lines of your property. One pool contractor I worked with wanted to position the waterfall right at the end of the pool, near the back fence, where he'd have maximum ease of installation. I insisted it be moved toward the center of the pool, in line with the view from the back door. In siting a waterfall, keep in mind other views from the house—the kitchen, the second floor, etc.

If you build up a slope to install a waterfall, you will most likely need to add a retaining wall to support the rise. You can choose to disguise that wall with plantings

4 BASICS

OF DESIGNING WATER FEATURES

1. *Treat your water feature as an investment—and make it personal.* Water features will add a wonderful dimension to your landscape and, if done properly, increase the resale value of your property. If you can't afford a custom pool at the size you want, downsize rather than purchase one of the prefab pools on the market. Instead, create something customized to your needs and home.

2. *Talk with a variety of experts.* Pools—and to a lesser extent ponds, fountains and waterfalls—involve a variety of building codes, safety issues, wildlife concerns and other important elements you'll need to understand. Don't expect that your contractor will know anything about the local wildlife.

3. *Measure twice, cut once.* Proportions for waterfalls, ponds, swimming pools and fountains are critical. Use twine, a garden hose or a tarp to mark off the space for the planned pond, or erect a ladder at the height you feel is appropriate for your fountain or waterfall. Take one step back, then 30 steps back. See if the proposed project works well from a number of views.

4. *Integrate, integrate, integrate.* Make your water feature a seamless part of your hardscape. Terraces, walkways, decks and other hardscaping elements should flow into and from the water feature.

or design it so that it is 18" high and doubles as seating. This is a good way to reduce the amount of furniture you'll need on your patio area.

Opposite: Large boulders and plant material are introduced to create a seamless transition from waterfall to wooded background. **Above:** The water from a swimming pool in the background is used as a waterfall in the foreground before it is recirculated back to the pool.

METAL

Predominantly four types of metal are used in landscape development—steel, aluminum, copper/brass and ornamental iron—and in the hardscape, they most often take the form of fencing, railing or gates. Metal is found in either rustic or modern settings, and the patina it develops over time adds a layer of age and permanence to the setting. Metal needs no maintenance so long as you find rust or patinas charming. It's bug-proof, strong and comparatively low cost. Unless you're using metal for art or sculpture within the garden, it is more often found as a structural element to other hardscaping materials. Thus, it's most important to understand how to finish your ornamental metal to make it resist the elements.

When using metal in the landscape, you should also consider how to slow corrosion. Generally, when two different metals come into contact with each other, a reaction often occurs that will begin the corrosion process. You should use a rubber or plastic separator to prevent contact. For instance, if you're fastening a steel U-bolt to an aluminum post, a rubber insert will help preserve both metals. Alternatively, wherever metal comes into contact with wood, it's always a good idea to treat the wood. So if you're fastening a metal bracket to a piece of wood, use CCA to make the wood weather resistant.

1.

2.

1. Metal art and sculpture have become more popular in the outdoor garden. They range from rough pieces of metal that frame paths to artistically crafted birdbaths. **2.** Since wrought-iron fences are custom made by a welder, you have the option of creating a design unique to your neighborhood.

3. The patina finish of weathered copper blends naturally with any garden setting and can be a great conversation piece. Always choose garden ornaments that have meaning to you and that work well with the landscape and architecture of your home.

4.

5.

6.

Metal Finishes

Painting or rust-proofing are the only DIY finishes the homeowner can apply to metals to help them withstand the elements. Once you start these processes, though, they normally become annual affairs. As paint oxidizes, it will continue rusting. To avoid rusting, check also for these types of finishes when buying your metals:

- **Galvanized:** This process is usually applied to steel. You'll commonly see it for chain-link fences, railings, nails, nuts and bolts, and pipes.
- **Cadmium-, nickel-, or chrome-plated:** Plating is often used on nuts and bolts and miscellaneous hardware items as rust-proofing.
- **Anodized:** Normally, this is associated with aluminum fencing to prevent rust or corrosion.
- **Machined:** You can get a matte, polished or satin finish by machining the metal.

PROS

1. It's a strong structural material.
2. It has a long life span.
3. It takes a wide variety of finishes.
4. It's easily customized to any shape.
5. Ornamental metal can add a different dimension to your hardscape.

CONS

1. Other than wrought iron, it can heat up and create a glare in direct sunlight.
2. Unless treated, it's prone to corrosion.
3. It's generally more expensive than wood.
4. It requires specialized labor for installation; any customizing needs to be done in a machine shop.
5. It has a high rate of expansion and contraction.

4. Metal is often used structurally and when paired with glass can create a sleek, contemporary look. **5.** Metal furniture is a good choice for seating. You may want to consider cushions, if appropriate, to add extra comfort. Green is an excellent color choice for metal garden furniture.

6. Art comes in many forms. When selecting lighting fixtures, consider ones that will add intrigue to your exterior garden room.

GLASS

Many of us have a glass tabletop on our patios, and that's where this material usually remains. Used in measured doses, however, glass can be very effective in the hardscape. Take advantage of its translucency and ability to reflect light. It's not unusual to see bits of colored glass embedded in concrete retaining walls, outlining fishponds, or in ornamental applications. Glass can also be used in railings or as shields against the wind, acting as a barrier without closing off light and views. For roof extensions, you can also use glass to create skylights that won't close off light into interior spaces. And for areas with views underneath (i.e., a small creek running under a deck), strong, engineered glass can be used as a paving material.

Mirrors work their magic outdoors as well as indoors; they make small areas seem larger and dark areas seem lighter. If your ambitions run to rows of hedges and wandering pathways, mirrors can create surprises and illusions for the traveler. Glass stands up well to weather but won't bear weight. Also, avoid installing mirror or glass near soil, where it will catch splatters and dust, requiring constant maintenance. In the landscape, you'll want to use tempered glass that will shatter upon impact like a car window. A crack in plate glass can leave big, dangerous shards.

1.

1. The rear of a house is the perfect place to create an enclosed garden space. Glass walls establish a strong outdoor connection while keeping all of the benefits of indoor areas. **2.** Glass tabletops tend to work well in settings with a formal tone.

PROS

1. Tempered glass is generally safe.
2. It can be tinted in various degrees of darkness, frosted, given different types of designs or stained, with decorative finishes.
3. Because it is a manufactured product, you can purchase it in virtually any dimension to suit your needs.
4. It's easily customized to make curves and other shapes.
5. Privacy can be created with one-way glass that promote views from only one side.

CONS

1. It can shatter and needs to be clear of play areas.
2. Engineered or customized glass can be expensive.
3. Specialty hardware and labor are required to fasten glass to wood.
4. Constant maintenance is required: Just like your windows, exterior glass needs to be cleaned regularly.
5. Because of its transparency, visitors may not be aware glass is there there and bang into it.

3.

2.

3. Glass can make strong connections between the home and the landscape. It is a great solution when you are looking to enhance the ground-level outdoor experience on a raised deck or porch.

PLASTIC

In the landscape, plastic is most commonly found in drainage conduits, outdoor furniture, potting accoutrements or other accessories, although there are a few innovative ways to incorporate this material elsewhere. Opaque sheets of plastic, in fact, can be effective screens for privacy. At night, these screens can be back-lit to cast the silhouette of adjacent plant material onto the screen. (See Chapter 6, *Decorating Outdoors*.) Thin sheets of tinted plastic can also be incorporated into wood or stone partitions, again using candles or other forms of illumination to create warm and subtle light in an outdoor room. In various contours, moulded plastic can be used overhead to create shelter from sun and rain. Plastic can also act as inexpensive supports or posts. There are many decorative plastic columns that, when painted, have the appearance of a wood finish. Most of these types of columns usually wrap around a wooden or steel post and are solely used for decorative purposes.

1.

2.

1. Plastic furniture design has come a long way with the innovative technology available today.

2. Translucent sheets of plastic act as a windscreen for this balcony garden. In the nighttime, they are back-lit to create a soft, subtle glow. The lights and view of the downtown skyline create a perfect space for romantic entertaining.

3.

PROS

1. It's generally less expensive than wood, stone or glass.
2. You can apply any color or painted finish to it.
3. It can be molded into any number of custom shapes and sizes.
4. It can be very decorative (i.e., columns).
5. It's easy to install.
6. It has a long life span.

CONS

1. Because of its light weight, it's not a good structural component and has to be secured.
2. Like glass, you may need to clean it regularly.
3. It can disfigure in extreme heat and will also get hot quickly.
4. Because of its manufactured nature, it has limited applications outside.
5. Plastic components, such as hose fixtures, can wear down with regular use.

4.

3. Light weight and easy storage make plastic garden furniture a very flexible alternative. It can come in numerous colors and is very cost-effective. **4.** Consider how often you entertain and how large your parties are when choosing a patio set. Large or small, purchase a set that suits your garden and meets your needs.

CHAPTER 6

DECORATING OUTDOORS
GARDEN FURNISHINGS & LIGHTING

Well thought-out placement of furniture and ornament is essential to any landscape. A statue or a bench at the end of a walkway draws the eye, guiding you visually and serving as punctuation as you move through a garden

space. Likewise, strategic arrangements of chaises, benches, tables and chairs offer points of interest that can either be displayed in the open or revealed as you enter various areas, or rooms, of a garden. This type of exterior decoration acts as a bridge between the landscape and the interiors of the house.

Whatever the style of the house—Georgian, Italianate, Victorian—the garden furniture and accessories are opportunities for you to extend your personal style. Objects such as urns or chairs add an immediate sense of scale and a human element to what might otherwise be an under-utilized space. By the same token, well-designed lighting can create wonderful moods that can transform an outdoor space. When lit well, garden areas can seem like two very different spaces—one during daylight hours and another, quite different one, once the sun has set.

Rebecca Coles, a garden designer and host of TV's *Surprise by Design*, likens hardscape to the architecture of a home and softscape to its interior design. I would take that analogy a step further and include garden furniture, accessories and lighting as the "interior design" of your outdoor room. Once you've established the basic outdoor structure with your hardscape, the real fun begins. Your garden furnishings and lighting, as well as the surrounding softscape, will create distinctive atmospheres and moods that will help you personalize your space.

Opposite: A simple window box treatment and a piece of sculpture can be all that's needed to accentuate the garden. Remember to consider complementary color in your plant selections. **Right:** Simplicity is often best when choosing outdoor furniture. This cast-iron table set blends easily into its natural setting.

FURNISHINGS

Finally it's time to take a seat. The question is, What kind of seat? Making a selection of outdoor furnishings is similar to picking out furniture for any room of your home. You have to consider space, light and function. And of course, furniture has to fit the body. Not every six-foot-

Rustic choices often work best in the outdoors. This old, stained cedar
bench blends into its landscape and calls for company. Its well-worn
facade gives it undeniable character.

A detailed birdhouse, complete with a chimney, echoes the architecture of the main house. Birds are drawn to birdhouses set among plantings.

tall man is going to be comfortable sitting for long on a Victorian wrought-iron fern bench.

What's different about decorating outdoors is scale. Your outdoor room is likely to be bigger than your indoor one. According to Joe Delgreco, owner of Delgreco & Company, a designer source for outdoor furniture, "Larger scale furniture is always better outdoors; because nature is so vast, smaller items get lost." If you're choosing furniture for sweeping lawns and spacious terraces, the scale of your furniture can be correspondingly larger. You can sprinkle chaises and settees here and there, keeping in mind that if the furniture doesn't have the kind of solid arms that are traditional to Adirondack chairs, your

guests will need a stable surface on which to rest a drink or a book. That surface can be a small decorative chair, a pillowed ottoman or a weathered wooden stool.

Exterior pieces also need to have strong silhouettes. They work in the landscape like sculpture. John Danzer, owner of New York's high-end garden furniture shop Munder-Skiles, points out that exterior furniture is rarely pushed against a wall. "Inside, we look at tabletops rather than bases," he says. "Outdoors, we tend to be very conscious of the table bases and proportions, so the base must look stable."

As in indoor rooms, you'll need to carefully consider how you plan to use your spaces. You'll want seating

in spots where you want to contemplate your garden. It's helpful to make a list of all the views you want to admire and then make sure that there's a chair or bench handy for each, assuming you haven't already designed a wall to rest on as part of your hardscape. Since outdoor areas tend to be places for meditation, you should consider how your furnishings can enhance those experiences. Will you be alone with your thoughts or will you be settling in with a spouse and a glass of wine? Will you want to be sitting upright or reclining in a hammock?

Paying strict attention to function is especially critical when you're furnishing a city patio or a small terrace. There's nothing worse than tripping over chair legs, whether you're indoors or out. In smaller spaces, you may not be able to have a table that sits twelve or display a dinner party's worth of chairs on a regular basis. When figuring out your furniture plan, it's best to design for intimate use, for family dinners and Sunday breakfasts. You can always add folding tables and chairs as needed. In many cases, if you're having a dinner party, you can bring your indoor furniture outside. When a gateleg table or ladder-back chairs are brought outside, an outdoor party feels like a true occasion.

Color

Color will transform how your garden furniture looks. The general rule is that lighter shades will come forward and look larger, whereas darker hues will recede and look smaller. White is, of course, the lightest of colors and the shade most likely to make your furniture scream "look at me," especially when it is set against the green tapestry of your lawn. As Gertrude Jekyll politely put it a century ago: "The common habit of painting garden seats a dead white is certainly open to criticism. The seat should not be made too conspicuous." If you do want white, avoid a stark, bright hue. Pure white creates glare and casts crisp shadows. Off-white is soothing to look at

and casts shadows that are not as harsh and cold. (Of course, white is also the most difficult color to maintain; if your outdoor room receives a lot of mud splatter from adjacent grass or planting bed areas, you may want to consider a different color.)

If not off-white, what color? Natural wood is a choice guaranteed to make furniture blend in with your garden. Black and dark green will harmonize rather than compete with plantings. Silvery grays, turquoise and sky blues, and muted beiges are also good choices. Rosemary Verey, the great British garden designer, describes in *Classic Garden Design* a shade of deep green that is "so dark you have to look twice before you realize it is not black. It is a safe colour to use in almost all circumstances."

If you want to make a piece of furniture stand out, consider a fabulous yellow or bright primary color. If you

Opposite: Comfort is inherent when you have chosen the right furniture for your garden. Remember scale: The furniture should be in proportion to the size of your garden room. **Above:** Dark greens are a safe choice for textile and furniture selections.

prefer to come upon a chair or a bench unexpectedly, stick to neutrals. Remember that, exposed to the sun and rain, colors are likely to weather and mellow as the years go by.

Fabrics

Since many chairs need cushions, what fabric do you choose? A general rule of thumb is to avoid anything too vibrant. In the outdoors, nature should reign. Keep the most strongly patterned seats near the house so they won't compete with your plantings and vistas. As with strong color, strong pattern attracts the eye and fore-

shortens space. And remember that an abundance of pattern makes spaces feel smaller.

Pattern does have its place. On a deck or terrace, pattern can carry the theme of your interior decorating outside. It can be playful—bold stripes can echo a slatted fence—and very flattering, especially if it echoes the colors in your flowers or place settings. If you aren't planning to tote cushions in and out, choose fabric that is weatherproof—colorfast, mildew resistant and able to stand up to wet bathing suits.

Flexibility

Unlike your indoor environments, nature is not static. "An exterior decorator," says John Danzer, "has to work in an ever-changing world with infinite space, open horizons, changing seasons, falling leaves and growing flowers." Given these circumstances, he doesn't believe in making a hard-and-fast floor plan for the garden. "The furniture will be moved around depending on the season and the type of event that takes place," he says, "so portability and flexibility tend to be the most important features to consider."

At the end of a summer day, your furniture is likely to be in a very different place than where it started out in the morning. "No guest would dare rearrange the furniture in your living room, but outside the rules are different," says Connecticut landscape designer Janice Parker. "Everyone wants to get just the right quality of sunlight or just the right bit of shade. You need to realize this aspect of designing outdoors and plan accordingly."

If the furniture you choose for outdoor gathering spaces is lightweight, your guests will thank you (so will the person who mows your lawn). And if you live in a climate where furniture can't be left outside all winter, you'll appreciate lightweight chairs when it comes time to stack them in your garage or garden shed.

Above: When selecting fabrics, remember to ask for exterior grade quality. Your garden furniture will look better and last longer after seasons of rain and snow. Manufactured by Kingsley-Bate. **Opposite:** Although fairly heavy, an Adirondack chair is still a flexible choice for this sort of setting. You can use the runners to drag it to the best view.

DESIGN TIP

Antique garden furniture is often an overlooked and inepensive collectible that can be found at auctions or even on eBay. The trick is to make sure weather hasn't taken too much of a toll on the furniture. Tables should be upended to make sure there's no rust or damage underneath. Bases need to be carefully inspected to make sure they're stable. Use a soft wire brush to smooth the surface of peeling paint. A mix of fleamarket chairs for an outdoor table can be unified with a single coat of paint.

Hardscape Furnishing Ideas

Classically, stonewalls or retaining walls have been used by landscape designers to double as benches. If they're designed to be standard chair height—18"—they'll work well for a tête-à-tête, but three or more people will have trouble carrying on a conversation while sitting in a straight line. If you're counting on a wall as seating in an area where there are no portable chairs to pull up to make a seating triangle, your best bet is to design walls or benches so they form an angle or an alcove.

If you want to create furniture out of stone, consider building benches and tables by taking two or three stone pedestals and laying a large piece of flagstone across them. A boulder can also double as a seat. Booher and Burdick are masters at selecting beautiful boulders from the blueberry barrens near their office on Mount Desert Island, Maine. They've even created a stone sitting area with an amply proportioned boulder they call a stone couch. "The sitting area disappears right into the landscape," says Booher.

Above: This decorative Luyten's bench is made from high-quality, durable Balau wood. If you buy a Lutyen bench made from teakwood, remember to always ensure that the wood is from official teak farms and not the rain forest. Manufactured by Avonlea Gardens.

Chinese Chippendale: With its decorative back echoing lattice, this has been the perennial choice of gardeners at English country estates.

Adirondack chairs: Amply armed and slat backed, it was patented in 1905 as the Westport chair but became associated with the rustic charm of the Adirondacks.

Lutyens bench and chairs. The English architect Edwin Lutyens designed this furniture for the gardens he worked on with Gertrude Jekyll. Made of teak, it has a gracefully curving outline, slatted back and rounded, slatted arms. Available at many garden furniture companies, it is still enormously popular today.

Steamer chairs. If you can't board a luxury liner, these reclining chaises can at least line your pool. Some varieties fold flat and make handsome tables for parties. Make sure you buy a pair—they look best in two's.

French bistro chairs. Found at Parisian cafes, these chairs are not usually weatherproof but can add an elegant element to gardens.

Willow and twig chairs: These rustic choices captured the fancy of influential Victorian designers like Fredrick Law Olmsted and Andrew Jackson Downing.

Wicker: Wicker's golden age was the late nineteenth century, when fanciful furniture was any manner of pliable reeds. Wicker is actually a loose term for any furniture woven of rattan, reed, cane, willow, raffia, twisted paper or dried grass.

From top to bottom: (1) Chinese Chippendale style furniture like this rarely requires covering. Here, an angled-back design makes the chair and bench look larger than they really are. Manufactured by Kingsley-Bate. (2) Pool lounges, or steamers, will require comfortable cushions. If you buy a steamer made with teakwood, get it with built-in wheels—teak is a dense, heavy material. Manufactured by Kingsley-Bate.

(3) These teak steamer chairs bring a sense of nostalgia to a waterfront setting. They also fold away easily for storage. Manufactured by Smith & Hawken. (4) Wicker, although not as common in contemporary landscapes, remains a popular choice. Manufactured by Smith & Hawken.

Materials & Maintenance

When purchasing outdoor furniture, durability and maintenance are critical. Salt air, rain, mildew, chlorine from pools and the bleaching effect of the sun are all enemies of even the sturdiest furnishings. Which means that if you love the look of chairs that have blue and white striped cotton canvas pillows, you have to consider how much you'll love lugging the pillows inside every time the weather turns threatening.

Wood: It is not the thickness of the wood, but rather its density and water content that are important for the durability of wood furniture. Using hard redwoods, such as teak, cedar and mahogany, that have a natural resistance to water and decay and turn gray with age, is hugely popular for outdoor furniture. Many companies manufacture extensive lines of teak benches, chairs and accessories for the garden. Unfortunately, teak and other redwoods tend to be very expensive. Less costly lumber, such as pine, can be made resistant to decay by coating it with various chemical treatments. Such treated woods can be oiled, stained or painted using specialty products. Outdoor furniture made from these softer woods usually needs a fresh coat of wood preservative each year to resist rotting.

Wrought iron: A byproduct of the industrial revolution and the Victorian imagination, wrought iron is an

exceptionally durable option for outdoors. However, it is hard to sit on and heavy, which makes it unsuitable to use for dining chairs that need to be scooted in and out. It is also not a good choice for casual lawn furniture that will need to be shifted around during the day to follow the sun. When left out in the elements, antique wrought iron will also rust. Even newly painted metal furniture will eventually peel and need refinishing.

Aluminum furniture: Whether cast, tubular or wrought, aluminum furniture offers numerous advantages over iron, as it is non-rusting, easily maintained and lightweight. Aluminum maintains its appearance in the elements, and many designers like its silvery color in the garden.

Stainless steel: Another option is stainless steel—sleek, beautiful and durable. Like aluminum, stainless steel is a white metal resistant to corrosion; however, it has a higher weight-to-strength ratio, making it stronger than aluminum without the additional weight.

Natural materials: Wicker and rattan work well on porches or other covered areas. Despite their classic beauty, wicker and rattan will rot if left in continual exposure to the elements. Such furniture holds up beautifully against the elements during warm months and can be stored or covered in the winter.

Plastic: This material also has its place in the outdoor arena. Many common plastic chairs are shiny and cheap looking. But today, high-end companies are creating wonderfully sculptural pieces that are particularly welcome at poolside. Even ornate wicker is being recreated with woven strips of plastic resin.

Mixing It Up

Once upon a time, suites of furniture—sofas and matching chairs—reigned in living rooms across America. Today, we're accustomed to individualizing interior decorating schemes, though exterior decorating still relies heavily on the suite concept. Do you want your patio or lawn furniture to match exactly? If you're doing a retro look—1940s tropical leaves on bamboo chairs—the answer might be yes. But more often, today's garden rooms are decorated with carefully chosen individual pieces. Danzer says he often mixes and matches for clients: "It just depends on what fits the bill." For example, he might specify durable and easily maintainable furniture by the pool, and something more formal on the patio next to the house. And mixing doesn't only involve styles. Pairing wood with wicker or teak with aluminum can add texture to the garden.

Opposite: Plastic furniture is durable, cheap and increasingly stylish in design. **Top:** Stone is almost always a good material choice in the landscape, though not very flexible. **Bottom:** If you select finely finished wood furniture, make sure it will have appropriate protection from the elements.

Garden Ornaments

Garden ornaments can range from obelisks and urns to marble nymphs and abstract stabiles, from artisanal birdhouses to fanciful scarecrows, from old watering cans to apple-picking ladders. Like accessories in the house, garden ornaments are magical elements. They highlight axes and create focal points. They draw the eye and offer an invitation to wander and see what a particular corner might hold. But unlike interior accessories, garden ornaments must be considered in relation to the changing seasons. When trees shed their leaves and the garden dies back, they will naturally stand out.

"When we use garden ornaments," says Barbara Israel, owner of Barbara Israel Garden Antiques in Katonah, New York, "we connect them to the surroundings. That relationship to nature is extremely important to me: A birdbath reflects the sky and the water that fell from it; the bird—which is again the representative of nature—uses it. If we use a classical statue of a woman at the end of an allée, she'll represent a season or one of the elements and thereby represent nature."

Surprise is important when considering where to place ornaments. Garden designer Bunny Williams points out that a terra-cotta medallion from an architectural salvage company can be casually leaned against a tree. It might be set into a garden path, perhaps one of gravel, or hung on an exterior wall. It could also be used as decoration under a custom-made glass-topped table.

Sundials are often used to ornament the center of an herb or rose garden. Like birdbaths, they can be a focal point at the end of a garden. If they are vintage pieces and need a pedestal, make sure it isn't too tall. You want to be able to see the surface detail.

Other ornaments to consider: millstones, Gothic finials, decorative chimney pots, architectural fragments, even boulders. (The latter should be set carefully on an angle that directs your eye to some element in the garden.) When searching for these sorts of garden knick-knacks, be imaginative and trust a little in serendipity. If a well-priced item that doesn't have an obvious use catches my eye, I'll usually go ahead and buy it, then work out where it goes later. I find that these items often become true centerpieces.

Top: When selecting garden ornaments, first find something that has meaning to you, then find an area of the garden where it would be at home. **Bottom:** A terra-cotta urn can act as a focal point when planted and placed in the appropriate spot. **Opposite:** These sculptured herons look at home near the water's edge in the tall grassy plain.

Look to the architecture of the home when customizing lighting fixtures.
The fixtures here echo the windowpanes on the house.

LIGHTING

Lighting is essential to hardscaping—and not just because you need to guarantee that your guests won't trip as they climb your front steps. Night lighting creates character and romance, often making your garden feel even more magical at night than during the day. It shows off the bones of your garden and gives you a view to admire from inside your house as you wash dishes in your kitchen or host a party in your living room.

During winter months when nothing's growing, "you can lose your connection to the garden without landscape lighting," explains Jan Moyer, a professor at Rensselaer Polytechnic Institute's Lighting Research Center and a partner of MSH Visual Planners. "There's nothing more beautiful than a snow-covered garden, lit at night," she maintains. To enhance this sensibility, consider how lighting can facilitate an intimate walk through your landscape. You may not venture outside during a cold winter's night, but if you've created a lighting scheme that provides a quiet tour, up close and personal, it will also usually offer a stunning view from your window or the street.

Function, of course, is equally important, and you'll want to make sure that guests can get to their cars easily. "I'm amazed that even in multimillion-dollar homes, people will spend all this money and not think how to get down their stone steps at night," says Greg Yale, president of Greg Yale Landscape Illumination in Southampton, New York. Thus, planning for lights needs to coincide with your initial hardscape design. Whether you want lighting recessed in the steps or you're planning to illuminate the steps with the help of a down light in a nearby tree, you'll need to have your wiring in place before the masons arrive.

Most people light a path with freestanding path lights, but that is not the professional designer's first choice. As Jan Moyer points out, freestanding path lights

tend to get knocked by kids and snow shovels. And they are aesthetically unpleasing because they create glaring pools of light that contrast poorly with the darkness and actually weaken visibility. A better option: Hide a downlight in a nearby tree or add a downlight to a first-story eave and supplement it with lights hidden in shrubs, plantings or trellises. "Any time you can take the light off the ground and put it up where you won't see the brightness of the lens, you'll have more comfortable, effective lighting," says Moyer.

Path lighting is only one form of night lighting. The outdoor standing lamp is a safe and unique alternative to its indoor cousin. Designed by Greg Yale Illumination.

Highlight exceptional areas of the house and garden. Here, the designer chose to showcase the grand entrance to the home with multiple lighting sources.

Outdoor Lighting Tips

Plan for more junction locations than you think are necessary. Right now, you may just want to light one terrace or sculpture. But your trees—and your garden ambitions—will grow in ways you can't predict. So keep these pointers in mind:

• **Plan to put as many fixtures as you can on separate switches.** When you take the garbage out, you'll want task lighting. But when you're having a party, you'll want to keep the trash shed in the dark. Lighting—or lack thereof—can help you erase play sets, compost bins, storage sheds and anything else you don't want seen.

• **As in interior lighting, rely on dimmers.** First, you'll want to adjust your lighting intensity as the seasons change. When trees are leafed out, you may need more brightness. Second, when you're inside the house looking out, your exterior lighting will have to be bright or your windows will read as dark planes of glass. But when you go outside, you'll want low-level lighting to maintain nocturnal moods.

• **Don't overlight.** "It's so much more beautiful to have shadows and patterns and pockets of darkness," explains Yale. "The eye is always drawn to light. And the area between lights will be so much more interesting if it falls into darkness." The lighting designer's rule of thumb: Plan your lighting and then take away one fixture. Less is usually more outdoors.

• **Don't floodlight entertaining areas.** Yale describes an elaborate party he attended that left most of the guests trapped in a glare: "There were six 500 quartz floodlights coming down on a party filled with votive candles." A better solution would be to create the effect of moonlight. Light the terrace softly from above and supplement with lights in shrubs, or try a light that is a signature to Yale's firm: an outdoor version of the standing floor lamp, complete with a white shade.

From top to bottom: (1) Exposed copper light fixtures will develop a beautiful green patina over time. (2) Mounted light fixtures hide the bulb while safely illuminating stairs. (3) Select path lights that complement nearby planting. (4) Wall lighting is a great technique to illuminate plantings and create interesting shadows and patterns.

• **Pick a focal point—or two or three.** It might be a series of statues, the intriguing shape of a trellis or arbor or a selection of stunning specimen trees. Light all these with your brightest lights. Then balance the composition by lighting shrubs or secondary focal points with lower-wattage lighting. "The primary focal point should be five to ten times brighter than the secondary focal point," says Moyer. The thing that requires the least light: the lawn.

Hide exterior light sources where possible. At the end of the day, the light created is more important than its source. This is especially true if your home has a lot of glass, as the light created in the house will also illuminate the landscape.

• **Take into account seasonal changes to your garden.** "As the fullness of the garden goes away, you get a much deeper view," says Moyer. "The garden feels more expansive. Plan to light different features in different seasons."

• **Make sure fixtures are louvered and shrouded.** You don't want to be able to look into the bright hot spot of a bulb.

• **Aim for "moonlighting."** This technique is created by several low-wattage lights placed in a tree. The shadows they cast and the patterns they create on a lawn or paved terrace replicate moonlight.

• **Experiment with "grazing."** Use uplights to highlight the texture of the stone façade of a house or a particularly interesting stone wall. The lights "graze" the stone, shining vertically.

• **Buy good quality fixtures.** If you can, shop at specialty lighting stores rather than hardware or lumber stores. You may pay more for fixtures, but they need to be top quality to resist corrosion—and the impact of wayward bikes and shovels. "The outdoor environment is extremely destructive," says Moyer. "You want a fixture that will last."

• **Plan pool lighting to avoid glare.** Although pool lighting will probably be installed by your pool contractor, double-check to make sure that the sunken lights are not on the wall facing your house, or you'll be looking out into underwater glare.

• **Light decks under steps and handrails.** A number of specialty lights are on the market for lighting decks and steps for safety and nighttime use. Disk lights installed on railing support posts will wash a deck with soft light.

• **Light yourself a secret garden.** By day, you may not be able to create a perfectly secluded space, but by night you can let darkness envelope a remote seating area so that you feel perfectly hidden away. No one but the crickets will know.

1. *Establish a sense of enclosure.* Create walls (with trees, shrubs, fences and stone walls), develop a floor (with flagstone, interlocking stone, brick, gravel, concrete and other materials) and establish a ceiling plane (with trees, arbors, trellises or awnings) to make your outdoor space feel like an outdoor room.

2. *Remember your surroundings.* Select and place furniture (teak, aluminum, wrought iron) that integrates well with both the house and outdoor environment.

3. *Think through all four seasons.* Accessorize with furnishings, garden ornaments, potted plants and other items that can be changed with each passing season.

4. *Don't shortchange the nocturnal experience.* Light the space to make it a warm and inviting space at night, when most of us are home and able to spend quality time outdoors.

• **Don't forget the power of candlelight.** Bring out a candlelit chandelier, and hang it from a tree or underneath an outdoor dining-table umbrella; line a path with luminaria (white lunch-type bags filled with sand and a sturdy plumber's candle); around an arbor, set hurricane lamps on steps; fill seashells with votive candles. Nothing mingles better with starlight than candlelight.

RESOURCES

Resources are one of the most important aspects of landscape design. There are literally tens of thousands of vendors, artisans, suppliers, manufacturers and retailers out there. In this appendix, you'll find a selection of the

authors' favorites. Please note that many of the listings have multiple locations. Due to limited space, we've usually included the contact information for the U.S. headquarters only, or where applicable, Canadian headquarters. Please call the vendor directly for a location or supplier near you. Also many of the sources listed sell to the trade (architects and designers) only. If you aren't working with an interior designer or architect, you may be able to get a contact number from the vendor of a design service that may purchase the items for you.

PROFESSIONALS

Landscape Architects & Garden Designers

Ashley Christopher
Robert AM Stern Architects
460 West 34th Street
New York, NY 10001
T: 212.967.5100
a.christopher@ramsa.com
Landscape architect at leading architectural firm.

Austin Tao & Associates, Inc.
Austin Tao, FASLA
21-01 Locust Street
St. Louis, MO 63103
T: 314.436.3999
www.austintao.com

Burdick & Booher, ASLA
Bobbie Burdick &
Jennifer Steen Booher
33 Ripples Road
Mount Desert Island, ME 04660
T: 207.244.7663
www.burdickandbooher.com

Cole Creates
Rebecca Cole
41 King Street
New York, NY 10014
T: 212.255.4797
Garden & interior designer, author and host of TV's *Surprise by Design*.

Daniel Sherman, Landscape Architect
33 W. 17th Street, 9W
New York, NY 10011
T: 212.727.0999
Landscape architect specializing in incorporating pools into the hardscape.

Dargan Landscape Architects
Mary Palmer Dargan
PO Box 11730
Atlanta, GA 30355
T: 800.454.3889
www.dargan.com
Landscape architects & master planners.

DTR Associates
7185 Chagrin Road, Suite A
Chagrin Falls, OH 44023
T: 440.247.2662
dtrassociates@core.com
Award-winning landscape firm.

Earl L. Reeder II
Earl Reeder Associates
346 Jones Street
Dayton, OH 45410
T: 937.461.7753
Landscape architects.

Edwina vonGal & Company, Ltd.
11-17 43rd Avenue
Long Island City, NY 11101
T: 718.706.6007
Well-known exterior designer; author of *Fresh Cuts*.

Finesse Landscape Design
Eric Hagenbruch
PO Box 711
St. James, NY 11780-0711
Toll Free: 800.681.3463
T: 631.862.9007
1finesse@optonline.net
Landscape design firm specializing in natural landscapes.

Gunn Landscapes, LLC
Alec Gun, RLA
343 East 85th Street, 2nd Floor
New York, NY 10028
T: 212.998.7065
www.gunnlandscapes.com

Seferian Design Group
Haig Seferian
3380 South Service Road
Burlington, ON, L7N 3J5, Canada
T: 905.634.3110
www.seferiandesign.com
info@seferiandesign.com

Janice Parker
52 Wakeman Hill Road
Sherman, CT 06784
T: 860.350.4497
JPLAdesign@aol.com
Famed landscape designer.

John Jay Land Management
Jay Archer & Bill Meyer
282 Katonah Avenue #268
Katonah, NY 10536
T: 914.232.0399
Full-service landscape design.

John Russell
664 Bluff Park Road
Birmingham, AL 35226
T: 205.824.5281
www.johnrusselllandscapearchitect.com
Licensed landscape architect.

Jordan Honeyman Landscape Architecture, LLC
Joan Honeyman
1003 K Street, NW, Suite 840
Washington DC, 20001
T: 202.737.0451
Licensed landscape architecture firm.

HM White
130 West 29th Street, 9th Floor
New York, NY 10001
T: 212.868.9411
www.hmwhitesa.com
Comprehensive landscape architecture firm.

Madison Cox Garden Design
220 West 19th Street
New York, NY 10011
T: 212.242.4631
Top-end designer who travels the world to work on both private and public gardens.

Nancy McCabe Garden Design
PO Box 447
Salisbury, CT 06068
T: 860.824.0354
Renowned garden designer.

Natural Landscape Design
89 King Street W, Suite 3
Dundas, ON L9H 1V1
Canada
T: 905.627.1466
www.naturallandscape-design.com
Landscape design firm and
member of Landscape Ontario.

Orange Street Studio
Michael Schneider, ASLA
3252 De Witt Drive
Los Angeles, CA 90068
T: 323.874.3352
Recipient of an ASLA 2003
Design Merit Award.

R.S. Granoff Architects, P.C.
Robert Brehm, ASLA
30 West Putnam Avenue
Greenwich, CT 06830
T: 203.625.9460
www.granoffarchitects.com
Landscape architect.

Exterior Lighting Consultants

Cline Bettridge Berstein Lighting
Design Inc.
30 West 22nd Street
New York, NY 10010
T: 212.741.3280
www.cbbld.com
Award-winning lighting design
firm that works with the nation's
leading architectural firms.

Edward J. Casino Lighting Design
1620 School Street, Suite 102
Morago, CA 64556
T: 925.376.9497
www.ejc.com
Full-service lighting design and
consulting firm.

Francis Krahe & Associates Inc.
425 Bush Street, Suite 426
San Francisco, CA 94108
T: 415.834.1903
www.fkaild.com
Lighting consultant firm with
offices in San Francisco and Los
Angeles.

Landscape Illumination
Greg Yale
27 Henry Road
Southampton, NY 11968
T: 631.287.2132
Veteran lighting designer who
works on projects all over the
country.

Mulhern Consulting Engineers
321 South York Road
Hatboro, PA 19040
T: 215.293.9900
www.mulhernengineers.com
Consultants who provide quality
outdoor lighting solutions.

ASSOCIATIONS

American Concrete Institute
38800 Country Club Drive
Farmington Hills, MI 48331
T: 248.848.3700
Information on concrete structures.

American Fence Association
www.americanfenceassociation.com
Contractor referral services.

American Lighting Association
PO Box 420288
Dallas, TX 75342-0288
T: 800.274.4484
www.americanlightingassoc.com
Provides safety information and
referrals for lighting consultants.

American Institute of Architects
1735 New York Ave., NW
Washington, DC 20006
T: 800.AIA.3837
www.aia.org
Offers architect referral services.

American Wood Council
1111 Nineteenth Street, NW,
Suite 800
Washington, DC 20036
T: 202.463.2766
www.awc.org
Provides information regarding
national codes and standards.

Associated Landscape Contractors
of America
150 Elden Street, Suite 270
Herndon, VA 20170
T: 800.395.ALCA; 703.736.9666
www.alca.org
Serving exterior and interior landscape, maintenance, installation
and design/build contractors.

Interlocking Concrete Pavement
Institute
1444 I Street NW, Suite 700
Washington, DC 20005-2210
T: 202.712.9036
F: 202.408.0285
www.icpi.org
Referrals for interlocking stone
manufacturers and designers, as
well as DIY and maintenance
information.

National Asphalt Pavement
Association
5100 Forbes Boulevard
Lanham, MD 20706
T: 888.468.6499
www.hotmix.com

National Paint & Coatings
Association (NPCA)
1500 Rhode Island Ave., NW
Washington, DC 20005
T: 202.462.6272
www.paint.org
Advice on manufacturers and
uses of their specific products.

National Association of the
Remodeling Industry
780 Lee St, Suite 200
Des Plaines, IL 60016
T: 800.611.6274; 847.298.9200
www.nari.org
Network of people who work in
the remodeling industry.

National Ornamental & Misc.
Metal Association (NOMMA)
532 Forest Parkway, Suite A
Forest Park, GA 30297
T: 404.363.4009
www.nomma.org
Members cover a wide spectrum
of metalwork, from blacksmithing
to light structural fabrication.

National Spa & Pool Institute
(NSPI)
2111 Eisenhower Avenue
Alexandria, VA 22314
T: 703.838.0083

National Stone, Sand & Gravel
Association
1605 King Street
Alexandria, VA 22314
T: 800.342.1415
www.nssga.org
Represents the crushed stone,
sand and gravel industry.

Tile Council of America
100 Clemson Research Blvd.
Anderson, SC 29625
T: 864.646.TILE
www.tile-usa.com

MATERIALS

Concrete

Get Real Surfaces
121 Washington Street
Poughkeepsie, NY 12601
T: 914.452.3988
Creates anything out of concrete;
specializes in architectural
concrete for interior design
applications.

Moxie International
5710 Roseville Road
Sacramento, CA 95842
T: 800.356.3476
www.moxie-intl.com
Manufacturer of concrete
admixtures, sealers and water-
proofers.

RMC Pacific Materials
6601 Koll Center Parkway
PO Box 5252
Pleasanton, CA 94566
T: 800.227.5186
www.rmcpacific.com
Manufacturer and supplier of
concrete and aggregates.

Solomon Colors
9035 Laurel Crest Drive
Crestwood, MO 63126
T: 800.344.0572
www.solomoncolors.com
Manufacturer and supplier of dry
and liquid pigments for ready-mix
and concrete applications.

TXI
1341 West Mockingbird Lane
Dallas, TX 75247
T: 972.647.6700
www.txi.com
Manufacturer and supplier of
concrete and aggregates.

Versa-Lok Retaining Wall Systems
6346 Highway 36, Suite 1
Oakdale, MN 55128
T: 800.770.4525
www.versa-lok.com
Retaining-wall systems made
from concrete blocks.

Asphalt

Asphalt Institute
Research Park Drive
PO Box 14052
Lexington, KY 40512-4052
T: 859.288.4960
www.asphaltinstitute.org
Association of industry producers
and manufacturers that provides
information on asphalt products.

Hanover Architectural Products
240 Bender Road
Hanover, PA 17331
T: 800.426.4242
F: 717.637.7145
www.hanoverpavers.com
Manufacturer of asphalt pavers
and blocks.

Stone

A-Stone Inc.
300 Morgan Avenue
Johnston, RI 02919
T: 401.942.0870
www.astoneinc.com
Comprehensive site for over 100
different types of stone.

Allstone Quarry Products, Inc.
RR1
Schormberg, ON, L0G 1T0
Canada
T: 905.839.8491
www.allstonequarry.com
Creates custom limestone and
granite accents for the home.

Attia Quarry
6 Satchell Boulevard
West Hill, ON, M1C 3B4
Canada
T: 416.266.7351
www.attiaquarry.com
Quarriers of all sizes of limestone.

Buechel Stone Corp.
W3639 Highway H
Chilton, WI 53014-9643
T: 920.849.9361
www.buechelstone.com
Supplier of an array of stone for walls, walkways and pool areas.

Champlain Stone, Ltd.
PO Box 650
Warrensburg, NY 12885
T: 518-623-2902
www.champlainstone.com
Quarriers of natural building and landscaping stone; supplies residential products across the US.

Haddonstone (USA), Ltd.
201 Heller Place
Bellmawr, NJ 08031
T: 609.931.7011
www.haddonstone.com
Established in the UK, a leading manufacturer of ornamental and cast stonework.

The Stone Yard
2 Spectacle Pond Road
Littleton, MA 01460
T: 800.231.2200
www.stoneyard.com
User-friendly resource for all types and cuts of natural stone.

Wood

84 Lumber
T: 724.228.8820
www.84lumber.com
Distributor of diverse types of wood across the US.

Golden State Lumber
719 Southpoint Boulevard, Suite C
Petaluma, CA 94954
T: 707.769.0181
www.goldenstatelumber.com
Nationwide lumber distributor.

Hayward Lumber
10 Ragsdale Drive, Suite 100
Monterey, CA 93940
T: 831.643.1900
www.haywardlumber.com
Nationwide lumber distributor.

Parr Lumber
5630 NW Five Oaks Drive
Hillsboro, OR 97124
T: 503.614.2500
www.parr.com
Lumber distributor for the Northwest.

Wickes Lumber
706 North Deerpath Drive
Vernon Hills, IL 60061
T: 800.558.1232
www.wickes.com
Store locations across the Northeast.

Metal

Casson Lassard
174 Birch Avenue
Princeton, NJ 08542
T: 609.989.4700
The ultimate source for custom ironwork.

DeAngelis Iron Works, Inc.
305 Depot Street
PO Box 350
South Easton, MA 02375
T: 508.238.4310
Fabricators of custom metal work; specializes in planning, contract preparation and design.

RF Coble Metal Design
3525 Florence Boulevard
Florence, AL 35634
T: 256.7575.2714
www.coblemetalworks.com
Designers and fabricators of ornamental and structural metal.

Tiles & Pavers

Bomanite Corp.
232 S. Schnoor Street
Madera, CA 93639
T: 559.673.2411
A poured-paving system, Bonanite can be imprinted to look like any surface, in any color.

Country Floors
8735 Melrose Avenue
Los Angeles, CA 90069
T: 310.657.0510
www.countryfloors.com
America's premier tile distributor since the 1960s.

Matt Stone
PO Box 261239
Tampa, FL 33685-1239
T: 800.422.1288
www.mattstone.com
Supplier of pavers, stepping-stones and edgers.

Terra Designs Inc.
PO Box 913
Dover, NJ 07802
T: 973.328.1135
Art tile manufacturer of mosaics.

Vermont Specialty Slate, Inc.
PO Box 4
Brandon, VT 05733
T: 800.247.6615
www.vtslate.com
Supplier of slate tile and paving stones.

Wholesale Tiles & Accessories, Inc.
1902 Flagler Street
Tampa, FL 33605
T: 813.248.0455
Distributor of many tile lines, including Astra Tiles, a custom polished concrete product.

Brick

Castaic Brick Inc.
PO Box 8
Castaic, CA 91310
T: 800.CASTAIC
www.castaicbrick.com
Manufacturer of brick products.

Gavin Historical Bricks
2050 Glendale Road
Iowa City, IA 52245
T: 319.354.5251
www.historicalbricks.com
Supplier of antique bricks and cobblestones for driveways, walkways, floors and walls.

Midwest Brick Company
PO Box 160
Woodstock, IL 60098
T: 815.648.1360
www.user.mc.net/mwbrick.com
Manufacturer of brick pavers and retaining walls.

Saco Brick Company
195 North Street
Saco, ME 04072
T: 207.286.1733
www.sacobrick.com
Manufacturer of brick products, including retaining walls and pavers.

Triangle Brick
6523 NC Highway 55
Durham, NC 27713
T: 800.672.8547
www.trianglebrick.com
Manufacturer of brick products in a variety of colors, textures and sizes.

Terra-Cotta

Boston Valley Terra Cotta
6860 South Abbott Road
Orchard Park, NY 14127
T: 716.649.7490
www.bostonvalley.com
Largest manufacturer of architectural terra-cotta in the US; specializes in both restoration and new construction.

Queen Bee Studios
T: 519.826.7825
www.architbits.com
Handcrafted terra-cotta garden ornaments.

Superior Clay Corp.
PO Box 352
Uhrichsville, OH 44683
T: 800.848.6166
www.superiorclay.com
Manufacturer of terra-cotta products, including mailboxes and chimney pots.

Gravel

Alleco Stone
10401 South Miller Road
Buckeye, AZ 85326
T: 623.386.1148
www.alleco.com
Producer of a wide range of aggregate materials.

Greely Sand & Gravel
PO Box 430
Greely, ON, K4P 1N6, Canada
T: 613.821.3003
www.greelysand.com
Supplier of limestone and river-washed stone.

Rogers Group Inc.
421 Great Circle Road
PO Box 25250
Nashville, TN 37202
T: 615.242.0585
www.rogersgroupinc.com
Produces quality construction grade aggregates.

Interlocking Stone

Irwin Stone
601 East Gude Drive
Rockville, MD 20850
T: 301.762.5800
www.irwinstone.com
Manufacturer of interlocking stone and other stone products.

Paveloc Industries Inc.
8302 South Route 23
Marengo, IL 60152
T: 815.568.4700
www.paveloc.com
Manufacturer of concrete paving stones and retaining walls.

Uni-Group USA
4362 Northlake Boulevard
Suite 204
Palm Beach Gardens, FL 33410
T: 800.872.1864
www.uni-groupusa.org
Manufacturer of interlocking concrete pavers.

Unilock, LTD
287 Armstrong Avenue
Georgetown, ON L7G 4X6
Canada
T: 800.864.5825
www.unilock.com
Manufacturer of interlocking stone that also provides design ideas.

Flooring

Alison T. Seymour, Inc.
5423 West Marginal Way SW
Seattle, WA 98106
T: 206.935.5471
Distributes Bolon vinyl flooring
from Sweden—a durable, water-
proof material for poolside or
other outdoor applications.

KwikDek
T: 415.586.4431
www.deckbuilding.com
Interlocking wooden tiles with
plastic backing for patios, decks
or paths.

Fencing

American Wood Fences & Decks
1 Brightleaf Court
Simpsonville, SC 29680
T: 864.963.8889
www.building.com
Custom designed and handcrafted
wooden fences.

Bamboo Fencer, Inc.
179 Boylston Street
Boston, MA 02130
T: 617.524.6137
Manufacturers of bamboo fencing, gates, pergolas, trellises and
orchid houses; has catalog and
will ship worldwide.

Clinton Fence
2630 Old Washington Road
Waldorf, MD 20601
T: 800.323.6869
www.clintonfence.com
Metal and fence designer and
manufacturer.

Lott Fence
PO Box 1597
Round Rock, TX 87680
T: 512.244.6681
www.lottfence.com
Manufacturers of wooden fencing.

Metal Fabrication & Design
138 Hamilton Drive, Suite C
Novato, CA 94949
T: 415.883.3494
www.metalfabanddesign.com
Custom designers of ornamental
iron for fences, gates, railings
and balconies.

Glass

Hurricane Creek Stained Glass
PO Box 891
Gualala, CA 95445
T: 707.884.4693
www.hclampworks.com
Outdoor lamps and wall mounts
made with art glass.

Exterior Lighting

Allscape Architectural Landscape
Lighting
2930 South Fairview
Santa Ana, CA 92704
T: 714.668.3660
www.alllighting.com
Sleek outdoor lighting solutions.

Ardee Lighting
639 Washburn Switch Road
PO Box 1769
Shelby, NC 28151
T: 888.442.7333
www.ardeelighting.com
Unique down lighting solutions.

Ball & Ball
463 W. Lincoln Highway
Exton, PA 19341
T: 610-363-7330
Reproduction interior and exterior
lighting fixtures and lanterns in
many styles. Crafted using the
same techniques as the originals.

BEGA/US
1005 Mark Avenue
Carpinteria, CA 93013
T: 805.684.0533
An international company that
specializes in outdoor lighting
fixtures that are timeless in style
and built to endure.

The Brass Light Gallery
PO Box 674
Milwaukee, WI 53201-0674
T: 800.243.9595
www.brasslightgallery.com
Quality light fixtures with design
integrity. All made on site by the
company.

High Tech Applications, Inc.
3117 Route 10
Denville, NJ 07834
T: 973.328.2700
Reps a variety of high-end out-
door fixtures.

Lumenfly
122 West 22nd Street
New York, NY 10011
T: 212.741.5555
www.lumenfly.com
Fine handcrafted silk lanterns.

Quality Lighting
1600 Melrose Avenue
PO Box 1389
Franklin Park, IL 60131-8389
T: 847.451.0400
www.qualitylighting.com
Manufacturers of a diverse line of
outdoor lighting solutions, including accent, pathway and post-top.

Teka Illumination, Inc.
86 Gibson Road, Suite 3
Templeton, CA 93465
T: 805.434.3511
High-end fixtures of durable
materials such as copper, brass
and stainless steel.

WATER RESOURCES

Irrigation

Hunter Industries
1940 Diamond Street
San Marcos, CA 92009
T: 800.733.2823
www.hunterindustries.com
Manufacturer of irrigation equipment, including pop-ups, rotors,
sprinklers and valves.

K-Rain Manufacturing Corporation
1640 Australian Avenue
Riviera Beach, FL 33104
T: 561.844.1002
www.krain.com
Manufacturer of irrigation equipment, including sprinklers, sprays
and controllers.

Pools

Anthony & Sylvan Pools
3739 Easton Road
Doylestown, PA 18901
T: 800.366.7958
www.anthonysylvan.com

La Francois Pool & Construction
39 Columbus Avenue
Spring Valley, NY 10977
T: 845.356.7500

Reed Pools
4068 NE Ninth Avenue
Ft. Lauderdale, FL 33334
T: 954.564.5235

Water's Edge Pools
65 Commerce Road
Stamford, CT 06902
T: 203.323.9710
Provides a full range of pool
options for private homes.

Fountains

Henri Studio Inc.
1250 Henri Drive
Wauconda, IL 60084
T: 800.323.4764
www.henristudio.com
Designer/manufacturer of original
cast-stone fountains and statuary.

Kenneth Lynch & Sons
PO Box 488
84 Danbury Street
Wilton, CT 06897
T: 203.762.8363
Catalog of cast stone, lead and
bronze fountains.

FURNISHINGS

Outdoor Furniture

American Country Home
327 Main Street
Ames, IA 50010
www.bistropatio.com
www.americancountryhomestore.com
Outdoor and indoor furnishings.

Avonlea Gardens
4301-G Fortune Place
Melbourne, FL 32904
T: 800.238.0604
www.avonleagardens.com
Durable, high-quality indoor and
outdoor furniture.

Barlow Tyrie, Inc.
1263 Glen Avenue, Suite 230
Moorestown, NJ 08057
T: 856.273.7878
www.teak.com
Exceptional teakwood outdoor
leisure furniture. Trade only.

Brown Jordan International
9860 Gidley Street
El Monte, CA 91731
T: 800.745.4252
www.brownjordan.com
Collection of fine outdoor and
casual furniture.

Delgreco & Company
232 East 59th Street
New York, NY 10022
T: 212.688.5310
Designer source for outdoor
furniture.

Giati Designs, Inc.
614 Santa Barbara Street
Santa Barbara, CA 93101
T: 805.965.6535
www.giati.com
Original furniture designs with
fine lines of plantation-grown
teak furniture, market umbrellas
and textiles.

Janus et Cie
8687 Melrose Avenue
West Hollywood, CA 90069
T: 310-652-7090
www.janusetcie.com
Renowned for high-quality garden
and casual furniture.

Kingsley-Bate
7200 Gateway Court
Manasses, VA 20109
T: 703.761.7000
www.kingsleybate.com
Manufacturer of fine teak outdoor
furniture.

Loom Italia
(through Country Gear Ltd.)
PO Box 727
Bridgehampton, NY 11932
T: 631.537.1032

Mecox Gardens
257 County Road
Southampton, NY 11968
T: 631.287.5015
www.mecoxgardens.com
Unusual garden ornaments and
furniture. Online catalog available.

Munder-Skiles
799 Madison Avenue, 3rd Floor
New York, NY 10021
T: 212.717.0150
Fine period outdoor furniture.

Palecek
PO Box 225
Richmond, CA 94808-0225
T: 800.274.7730
www.palecek.com
Award-winning casual furniture.

Smith & Hawken
4 Hamilton Landing
Novato, CA 94949
T: 800.940.1170
www.smithandhawken.com
Provider of high-quality, garden
inspired furniture and products.

Treillage Ltd.
418 East 75th Street
New York, NY 10021
T: 212.535.2288
www.treillageonline.com
Designers John Rosselli and
Bunny Williams' garden furniture,
lighting and accessories.

Triconfort
200 Lexington Avenue
New York, NY 10016
T: 212.685.7035
www.triconfort.com
Modern outdoor furniture.

Garden Ornament

Archiped Classics, Inc.
315 Cole Street
Dallas, TX 75207
T: 214.748.7437
www.archipedclassics.com
Fine cast-stone urns, jardinières,
pedestal tables and garden ornaments.

Barbara Israel Garden Antiques
21 East 79th Street
New York, NY 10021
T: 212.741.6281
www.bi-gardenantiques.com
Specializes in fine antique garden
ornaments from Europe and
America.

Beacon Products, Inc.
8503 19th Street East
Sarasota, FL 34243
T: 941.755.6694
www.beaconproducts.com
Manufacturer of wrought-iron
landscape furnishings and outdoor lighting.

Elizabeth Street Gardens
1176 Second Avenue
New York, NY 10021
T: 212.644.6969
Offers a selection of high-quality
antique and reproduction garden
ornaments, including statuary,
fountains and some furniture.

Florentine Craftsmen
46-24 28th Street
Long Island City, NY 11101
T: 800.971.7600
www.florentinecraftsmen.com
Smart selection of antiques and
reproduction pieces.

Irreplaceable Artifacts
216 East 125th Street
New York, NY 10035
T: 212.777.2900
Wide variety of architectural
antiques, including rustic garden
statues.

Limestone Trail Company, LTD
4965 Christie Drive
Beamsville, ON L0R 1B4
Canada
T: 800.810.8223
www.limestonetrail.com
Manufacturer of pre-built cedar
gazebos, spa enclosures and pool
houses.

Michael Trapp
7 River Road, Box 67
West Cornwall, CT 06796
T: 860.672.6098
Antique dealer and garden
designer with a penchant for
oversized architectural elements.

EDUCATION

Clemson Certificate of
Accomplishment in Landscape
Design (CCLAD)
Mary Palmer Dargan
121 Lee Hall
Clemson University
Clemson, SC 29634
T: 864.646.2432
www.cclad.org
Seminar series for beginners.
Distance courses available.

The Landscape Design Series
Video Teaching Guides
Vocational Education Products
California Polytechnic State
University
San Luis Obispo, CA 93407
T: 800.235.4146
Educational video series.

ONLINE RESOURCES

www.builderspace.com
Architecture and construction
industry portal.

www.concretenetwork.com
Information on concrete, including concrete contractor referrals.

www.concreteproducts.com
Full service concrete buyers
guide.

www.stonelocator.com
Advanced search engine for
knowledgeable stone buyers.

www.servicemagic.com
Find contractors and home
improvement specialists.

Wicker set manufactured by Smith & Hawken.

INDEX

ACME LANDSCAPE DESIGN*
T: 416.461.2263
62 (4), 88, 90 (bottom left), 91
(1), 106 (1), 147

AJE PRODUCTIONS
Author Photo, Jacket

ALL SEASONS GARDENING*
T: 905.576.4972
91 (4)

AVONLEAGARDENS.COM
174

THE BEACH GARDENER*
102 (1)

**BETWEEN THE FENCES
LANDSCAPING***
T: 905.475.0999
3

BETZ POOLS
T: 905.640.1424
153 (bottom)

BRAVO CEMENT CONTRACTING
T: 416.578.2111
www.bravocement.com
48 (4,5,6), 51 (5,6), 52 (2,3)

BURDICK & BOOHER, ASLA
40 (all), 41 (all), 62 (1,2,3), 74
(3), 76 (2,3), 90, 107 (6), 118
(middle), 132 (3), 133 (5), 146,
161 (6), 183 (1,2,3)

CITY PLANTINGS*
T: 519.686.1820
14

**COUNTRY ESTATES
LANDSCAPING INC.***
T: 905.689.4970
132 (2)

**DAWLAND FARMS
& LANDSCAPING***
T: 905.262.4862
48 (1), 118 (middle)

ELIOT KAUFMAN
T: 212.496.9460
18, 39, 68, 159

ENTIRE LANDSCAPES*
T: 905.629.2583
90 (top), 144

EVER-GREEN LANDSCAPING*
T: 905.575.4322
105 (4), 107 (4), 135 (5)

GARDENS BY DESIGN*
T: 905.469.0052
48 (3)

GIB-SAN POOLS LTD.
T: 416.749.4361
132 (1), 154 (top), 155

GREEN APPLE LANDSCAPING*
T: 416.288.1499
91 (3)

GREG HURSLEY
Through the Lens Management
T: 512.302.9391
32, 71, 134 (3)

HOGAN LANDSCAPING INC.*
T: 905.640.8374
109

HOLT JORDAN
T: 202.737.0451
77

HORTICULTURALLY YOURS*
T: 905.358.8189
105 (5), 149

HUNTER INDUSTRIES INC.
36 (3,4)

INTERNATIONAL LANDSCAPING*
T: 905.876.3000
20 (bottom), 91 (5)

**JAN GELDERMAN
LANDSCAPING***
T: 905.689.5433
Back Cover, 178 (top)

JASPHOTO.NET
T: 410.695.0373
53, 77

KENT FORD DESIGN GROUP*
T: 416.410.4994
61, 72 (bottom), 84, 103 (6), 104
(1), 119, 142, 160 (2), 164 (2),
183 (4)

**KIM PRICE LANDSCAPE
DESIGN***
T: 416.993.5143
103 (4)

KINGSLEY-BATE
138, 172, 175 (1,2)

LEIGH CHRISTIAN
Through the Lens Management
T: 512.302.9391
51 (3), 72, 87

**MACKINNON WATERFALLS
& PONDS***
T: 905.876.2836
107 (5)

MARY PALMER DARGAN
17 (all), 74 (1), 122

MOODER HORTICULTURAL*
T: 519.669.4073
8, 117, 134 (2)

OASIS POOLS
T: 905.637.7711
154 (bottom)

ORANGE STREET STUDIOS
50 (1), 52 (1), 118 (bottom)

PARKLANE LTD.*
T: 905.887.5851
7, 15, 20 (top), 21, 65 (bottom),
82, 135 (6), 178 (bottom)

PAUL BARDAGY
Through the Lens Management
T: 512.302.9391
19, 48 (2), 58, 59, 70, 133 (6),
162 (2)

PERENNIAL GARDENS CORP*
T: 416.531.1461
55, 56, 164 (1)

RAIN BIRD CORPORATION
36 (1,2)

RICHARD FARON
181

RISI STONE SYSTEMS
T: 800.626.9255
128

**ROCK WOOD CASUAL
FURNITURE**
T: 905.842.6437
138 (1), 139 (4,5,6)

ROGER TURK
T: 360.871.2792
4, 26, 38, 42, 43, 44, 46, 50
(2), 57, 64, 66, 67, 74 (2), 77
(5), 85, 102 (2), 110, 127, 133
(4), 150, 158, 165 (both), 166,
180, 182, 184

SALIVAN LANDSCAPE LTD.*
T: 416.321.2100
Front Cover, 83, 145

SEFERIAN DESIGN GROUP
104 (2,3), 136 (1,2), 137

STEFAN BOLLIGER ASSOCS.*
T: 705.737.2142
103 (5)

SMITH & HAWKEN
170, 175 (3,4), 190

STREETPRINT
www.streetprint.com
126

TIM LEE
T: 860.355.4661
Front Cover, 6, 9, 10, 11, 12, 13,
54, 60, 63, 65 (top), 69, 78, 80,
86, 93, 94, 95, 100, 105, 106
(2,3), 108, 115, 120, 123, 124,
125, 129, 130, 140, 143, 148,
156, 157 (top), 166, 168, 169,
171, 173, 176, 177 (both), 179

TOM JENSEN LANDSCAPES*
T: 416.801.8656
89

TUMBER AND ASSOCIATES*
T: 519.941.3867
91 (2)

UNILOCK LTD.
74 (4), 75 (all images), 116 (all
images), 157 (bottom), 167

WILLIAM WEBB
T: 216.631.1987
24, 25, 29, 33, 35, 37, 76 (1),
79, 80, 96, 98, 102 (3), 112,
113, 114, 131, 160 (1,3), 161
(4,5), 163 (3)

ZONE SIX DESIGN BUILD LTD.*
T: 905.944.8668
1

** Landscape Ontario Horticultural
Trades Association Awards of
Excellence Winner. All award
winners courtesy of Landscape
Ontario, T: 800.265.5656.*